Strategies and activities for teaching and learning language through cooperative play

Jo Ann Olliphant

Sahmarsh Publishing

dedication

To my best friend and husband, Webb and parents, Glenn and Dorothy Manning, who gave me the belief, encouragement and support which made this book a reality.

acknowledgements

To my friends Mary Ellen Myrene and Dierdre McCrary (editors) and Steve Conelly (production manager). Illustrations by Edie Carlson.

copyright

ISBN 1-879725-00-2

Sahmarsh Publishing

Table of Contents

Games for Beginners

Games for the More Advanced

Sources

Annotated Bibliography

The majority of the games can be creatively tailored to serve multiple purposes, so don't limit yourself to the specific games listed under each topic.

Preface

Feeling good about my students' learning rate and retention in French is a relatively new experience for me. Prior to the fall of 1981, I had spent 15 years teaching French to children of various ages and, although the younger children thought French was more fun than the older ones, few of any age group made significant gains toward fluency. Finally, I was forced to admit that one does not automatically become an effective teacher simply through time and experience. I began a journey that has led me to write this book. I have learned many things along the way, including this: teaching is not a static art. Like learning, it is a continuing process of risk, discovery and change.

Prior to my epiphany, I had no understanding of the direct relation between my lack of growth and the poor progress of my students. The fallout rate after beginning levels was high. Among those who managed or were forced to hang in there, few attained even minimum proficiency. The majority of my students were bright. I knew I had to be at least partly to blame and wondered what I had done wrong or if I had done anything right. What and how should I change?

After a brief escape into administration I rededicated myself to teaching, but not before launching a search for new ways to build a better language-learning trap. I was certain someone must know something about teaching language that I did not know. On the chance that professional journals offered some answers (they had all been literary discussions for college professors last time I remembered looking) I delved into their fine print and discovered a world of pedagogical information which was news to me.

My first big discovery was James Asher and *Total Physical Response*. After only one book and a workshop I was a convert. Elated by my initial efforts with TPR in the classroom, I began investigating the method in depth. More information raised more questions, and eventually I was seeking answers from every field of learning. Beyond second language research and methodologies, I found important pieces of the truth in learning styles, cooperative learning, critical thinking, psycholinguistics and brain research, to name a few.

Immediately, my classroom became my laboratory to test those ideas. The many triumphs, as well as tragedies (we most often arrive at what works by figuring out what doesn't work), guided the writing of *Total Physical Fun*. The games and activities—some original (if there is such a thing) and some adapted from ideas given me by my students and workshop participants—manifest the fruits of my experience. I have entitled the book in honor of James Asher and *Total Physical Response,* the man and methodology that first inspired me ten years ago.

One of the first pieces of the truth I discovered is that students take more risks and learn more easily when they are involved and at ease than when bored or anxious. Another key discovery was that language is learned best when used as a tool for doing or learning something else. Without ample time or facilities for such valid pursuits as art, cooking or science, I turned to game-playing. I was flabbergasted with how quickly the students learned, how willingly they participated, and how well they retained. To boot, I had never had so much fun teaching!

Played cooperatively, games encourage a pleasurable and productive interaction between teacher and class, putting the teacher in the proper role of advocate, not adversary. Even more, games have a remarkable potential for helping people connect with each other to promote self-growth, self-knowledge, creativity and joy. Supportive play breaks down barriers among group members and promotes trust, sensitivity, cooperation and positive social skill-building. Such healthy interaction requires good communication, the essence of language.

Using This Book

Total Physical Fun is not intended exclusively for teachers who use TPR. The book is for every teacher who knows the power of play and especially for teachers who have never used games in instruction. In addition to describing the games, *Total Physical Fun* suggests specific ways you can animate the play to achieve maximum results with students of all learning levels and age groups. In this respect, it is unique.

The value of these games multiplied by their versatility and adaptability. Once you have an assortment of props and pictures, no special preparation is normally required. The games can be used in a wide range of classroom settings and have been designed and field-tested with all ages.

Some of the rules in *Total Physical Fun* may seem complicated, but their intricacy is often the element which enables students to lose themselves in the game, be less afraid to make mistakes, and to acquire language more rapidly.

The games are organized by degree of difficulty, progressing from those for beginning language learners to those for the more advanced. If, however, after trying a game, you find you have miscalculated your group's ability, refer back to the description for ways to make it more or less advanced. You will find a variety of alternatives for adapting each activity to the learner's age and skill as well as to the size of the group and the classroom arrangement.

Each game is listed by name, with three subheads: grammatical element(s) or subject(s) targeted, and the main functions the students are to perform (Listening Comprehension, Speaking, Reading or Writing) and the materials you will need. **Note that all games expect and teach listening comprehension, but it is only listed in the *purpose* subheading when understanding is the major or only goal.**

Personalize the Games

Remember that the games and activities need not be taken verbatim. You are very likely already using your own version of some. As in cooking, feel free to mold, mangle, and modify others to suit your unique teaching style and situation, as well as the specific needs of your students.

As you take the role of innovator, I invite you to share your experiences with and reactions to *Total Physical Fun*. I encourage you to write: Jo Ann Olliphant, 11004 111th Street S.W., Tacoma, WA 98498. Phone: (206) 584-7473.

Key to Icons

The square icons next to each game title provide a visual marker to help you locate games which teach a particular subject or grammar point. Refer to the subject and grammar index following the games for complete listings. If you don't find the specific grammar point you need, see *Phrases or Other Structures*.

Telling Time

Verb Conjugations, Infinitives

Spelling

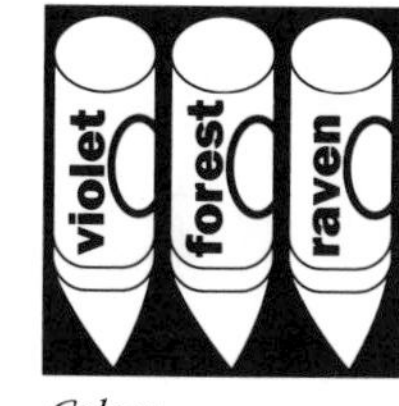

Colors

Questions, Answers

Nouns

Possessive Adjectives, Pronouns

Prepositions

Sentences

Cultural Information

Tense

Family, People

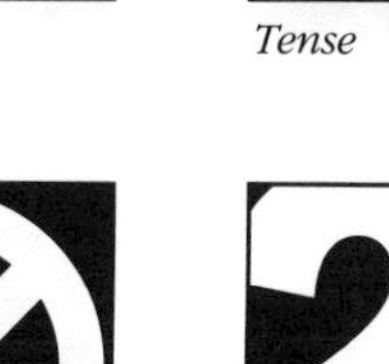

Alphabet

Negatives

Numbers

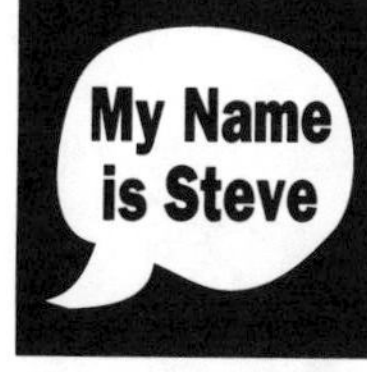

Names

Comparatives, Superlatives

Measurements

Body Parts

Adjectives

Adverbs

Commands

Phrases, Other Structures

Total Fhysical Fun

part 1 Total Physical FUNdamentals

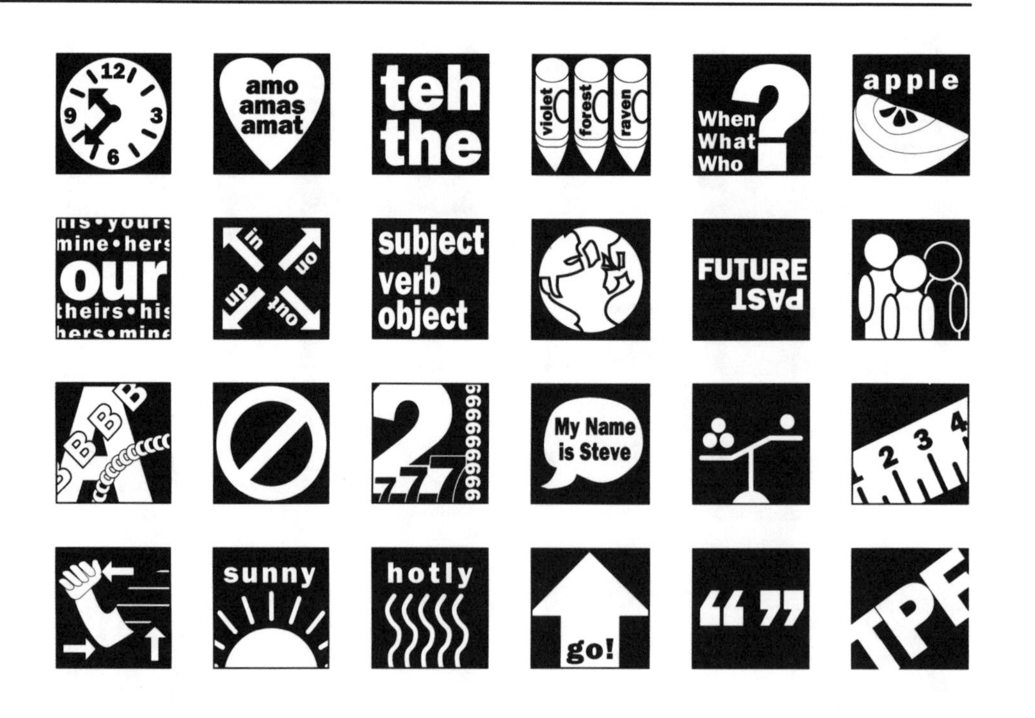

Total Physical FUNdamentals

part 1

Role of Games in Language Learning

Teachers who have tried TPR with great results sometimes become discouraged if student interest wanes after a few months. Any method used without sufficient variation to stimulate the brain becomes tedious. Understandably, students reject activities that are overly repetitive. Games provide a change in format and create the diversity needed to maintain interest with TPR commands. They also supply natural ways to introduce other language structures.

The games presented in this book should not be used merely as fillers at the end of the period or when the teacher and class need relief from the textbook. The games are designed for specific purposes, and those you select should be integrated into basic parts of the curriculum. Used properly, games can provide the vital link between the textbook and reality.

For most students, information in the textbook is not real until it is converted into meaningful activity. Textbooks mainly help students learn **about** the language – how it is put together. If the language is to be internalized, however, that knowledge must be used to transmit real messages. Using the language in ways that involve real communication is essential if the goal is fluency. Games can breathe life into possessive pronouns, the preterite and even the subjunctive!

Brain and learning research offer compelling evidence that play can speed learning and increase retention. Understanding why games work will help you animate and adapt the games more effectively. Here are some major points to keep in mind.

• Games help you to employ all of the five senses to facilitate memory. Each sense stores information in a different part of the brain. Retrieving or remembering becomes easier the more places the information is stored.

• The importance of real objects, pictures, movement and dramatization cannot be overstated. They are essential in stimulating the five senses (new neural connections are actually created) and convincing the brain that this information is real and should be stored.

• Although students often learn more quickly through games than they do through explanations and exercises, do not expect immediate learning. The brain seldom considers something important enough to store until it is encountered several times in several contexts. Any target vocabulary presented only once is not worth spending energy on. Some holiday activities fall in this category.

• The brain loves variety. Don't overplay one successful game. Alternate very active games with quiet games which require students to remain seated. Interchange activities which develop creativity with those that are drill-based. The change and variation helps students maintain focus and motivation.

• Finally, remember that students learn best when play is supportive and not overly competitive. For more on how to create a cooperative atmosphere, see *Creating a Stress-Free Environment,* in Part II.

If you are a teacher who apologizes for or conceals a penchant for playing games in the classroom, stop! Learning can and should be enjoyable. Even if games are boldly played **just for the fun of it,** learning cannot be avoided. Learners caught up in the spirit of play **want** to take part and are eager to understand, speak, read or write in order to continue the game. Because learning through play takes place with little direct effort, students often say, *It* (learning) *was easy.* Learning through play has thus become linked with easy. Some will argue that one cannot possibly learn without pain and anguish, so the idea of play in the classroom has often been rejected or done surreptitiously behind closed doors. You can now proceed openly and without guilt, because brain and learning research supply a convincing argument for teaching through play. You may still have to close your doors, however; enthusiastic language learners are frequently noisy.

Starting Out

With a Textbook

Teachers who work with an established textbook curriculum need to devise interesting ways to bring language structures off the printed page into the real lives of their students. Many of the games in *Total Physical Fun* invite use of any vocabulary or structure, so text material can be used in a variety of ways.

Teachers who begin with TPR may want to revise the order of textbook material so that the imperative comes first. Identify concrete nouns in the text and prepare a list of props and pictures you need. Extract vocabulary for oral work from upcoming chapters in advance of reading and writing. An oral foundation paves the way for student success. Many instructors delay using a textbook until after four months or longer.

Note that games and activities need not always be directly linked to the text. Supplemental material of high interest often motivates students to higher achievement on textbook work.

Without a Textbook

Teachers who build their own curriculum should keep in mind three principles of content for beginning courses: **(1) keep it common** (vocabulary and expressions used in normal, everyday language); **(2) make it interesting** (according to age and background of the learner); **(3) use the concrete** (tangible objects, verbs and structures which can be acted out). The more relevant, real and interesting you can make the material, the more rapidly and longer it will be retained in long-term memory. Games can play a central role in curriculum design. Once you have established what you wish to teach, select and adapt the games in this book.

Remember to keep an inventory of vocabulary and structures presented in order to facilitate review and recombination with material in successive lessons and games. Accompanying props and pictures provide excellent visual records of what you have taught or reminders of what you are going to teach.

Props and Pictures

Whether or not you use a text, most games in this book require an assortment of real objects and pictures. Props are essential to convey reality and facilitate learning. As much as possible, teach verbs which can be acted out and nouns for which you can find the objects or pictures. A foundation of concrete vocabulary provides a wealth of words to facilitate the later description and understanding of abstracts.

Remember that pictures are not limited to teaching nouns. They depict situations which may utilize verbs, adjectives and structures of all kinds. A picture card which must be seen by the entire group needs to be larger in size than a number flashcard.

Students are better able to recognize pictures from a distance if they have already encountered them at close range.

You can acquire a collection of real objects inexpensively if you utilize thrift shops, rummage sales, donations from students and parents, and things in your own home. For help in finding and making picture flashcards and objects, see the *Sources* section.

From Comprehension to Speaking, Reading and Writing

Understanding Before Speaking

You will notice that many of the games give you two options – to teach comprehension or speaking. In the beginning involve students in comprehension activities exclusively. Also, select the comprehension variation for introducing new material. Forcing students to speak too soon sets them up for failure because they cannot really hear or differentiate the new sounds until they have heard them many times. Constantly describe everything that takes place in all class activity, using repetitive, appropriate vocabulary.

Speech comes easily and naturally when students have spent sufficient time listening and responding physically. Some learners are ready to speak after about ten hours of instruction; others, especially children, require much longer. For further explanation of the comprehension or delayed oral response theory, see Asher; Krashen and Terrell, and Winitz, listed in *Annotated Bibliography.*

Avoid the pitfall of asking beginning students *to distinguish between* two words that sound alike, such as *sur* and *sous* in French. The difference between the two cannot be heard by most learners in the stage of early comprehension. This doesn't mean the teacher should not use similar words. Just try not to introduce sound-alikes together and remember that hearing the sound difference will take the students longer.

Once students begin speaking, they are ready to play the speaking variations of the games. Remember, however, that comprehension activities are still needed when new vocabulary is introduced. You will find that your students make the transition from comprehension to speaking rapidly as they become more advanced.

The Pros and Cons of Reading from the Beginning

Many of the games, especially in the beginning group, do not require reading. In later games, reading is often optional.

Reading aloud with poor pronunciation is a common occurrence in language classes. Students reading a language which uses the same alphabet as their first language will naturally employ the pronunciation systems which are well established in their brains. This naturally results in lots of mispronunciations. Reading may also be poor unless students have had sufficient opportunity to hear and use the words.

The teacher can reduce beginning speaking and reading errors by not focusing on the printed words. Students who initially only hear the words and do not see the spellings make fewer mispronunciations.

The drawback to withholding the written language is that many older learners become frustrated if they cannot see the words in print. In addition, since high school and adult learners already have extensive vocabularies, the spelling of a word may help them make an association for meaning, based on words they already know. These memory hooks are very valuable in retaining new material.

Younger learners, who have not developed a high dependence on the written word, will more likely be content with considerable oral development before the introduction of written words. This is one reason why students who begin a language in elementary school usually have pronunciation superior to those who begin in high school or as adults.

If you show your students the written words from the beginning, delay requiring them to speak the words until they have heard them correctly modeled and used many times (more than 50 for most learners). When poor pronunciation occurs, allow those students more listening time before asking them to respond again.

The teacher needs to make many oral repetitions of correct pronunciations when students work with a group of written words for the first time. As they read silently, many will *hear* the words, pronouncing them in their heads. If the correct pronunciation of the words they read has not yet been fully acquired, they will devise one, usually according to the sound/symbol connections they see in native language pronunciation. The faulty pronunciations which they practiced in their heads are very hard for most to correct, even if they recognize that what they hear the teacher say is not what they are saying. This occurs partly because few students are primarily auditory learners.

If you choose to delay presentation of the written language until after students are speaking, you may encounter resistance from older students who legitimately need to know what you are doing and why. The fact that your teaching strategies do not meet their expectations will interfere with students' motivation. To help deprogram their preconceived attitudes, give a presentation of the theory and evidence supporting an oral approach. See Asher and Winitz in *Annotated Bibliography.*

Pitfalls and Pratfalls

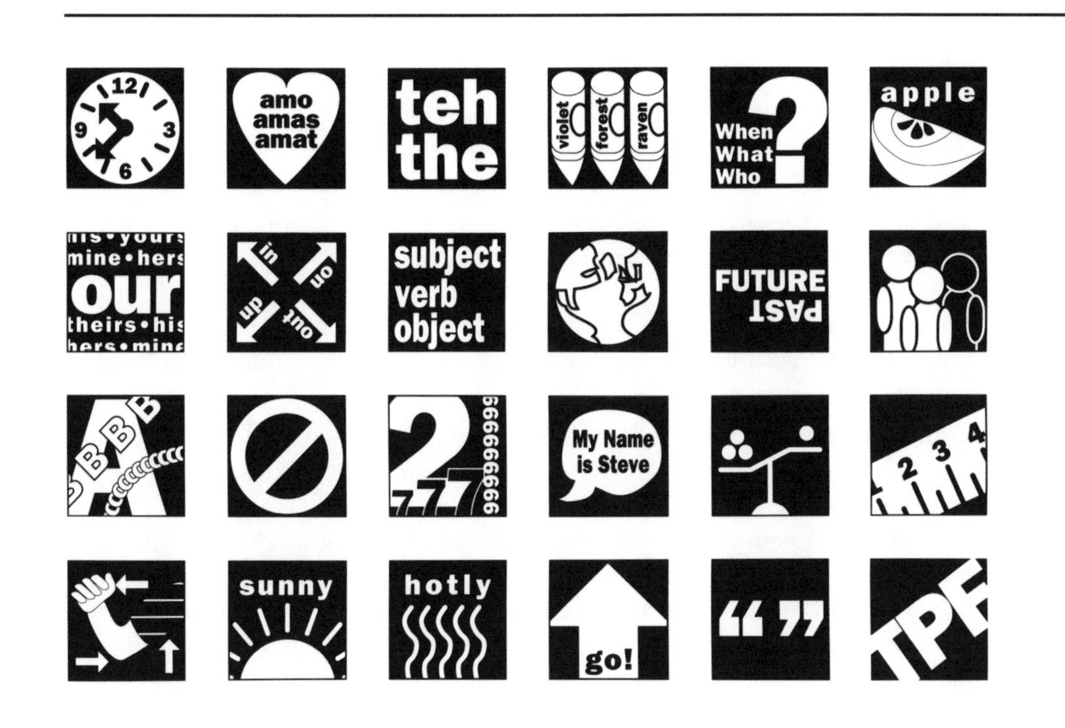

part 2 Pitfalls and Pratfalls

Getting to Know You

Why Choose Names in the Target Language?

Because names are an ideal way to learn new sounds and words, allow students to choose first names in the target language. Receiving new names is not recommended, however, for ESL students and very young children. They are usually new to the country or school and may find it threatening to give up their names.

In addition students can select last names, addresses and occupations, creating entire new identities for themselves. This role-playing is not only informative and creative fun but also serves the function of a protective mask, encouraging learners to take more risks, speak sooner and accelerate learning. A different name each year increases the number of words learned.

Since some students may resist role-playing at first, be flexible enough to make exceptions when necessary. It is important for beginnings to be positive.

Organizing the Name Selection

First Names

Secure a list of first names, preferably with sounds which are not too close to names that exist in the students' native language. Should there be someone in a French class named *Michelle*, for example, it is unwise to let her retain her real name. The difference in pronunciation from one language to another is minimal and because she and her classmates are so accustomed to saying *Michelle* in English, that pronunciation will be automatic.

Students who can read choose from lists of names. Make enough copies of the lists to allow one per student in your largest class. Each class can use the same set of lists. If you have several classes of students and don't wish to keep track of five different *Adèles*, do not allow students to pick names that have already been chosen in any other class. One way to prevent duplication is to have students in every class write their choices in alphabetical order on the board. Write *A* to *Z* headings, leaving space for students to fill in their names. Omit those letters which do not begin names on your list. Students in successive classes are instructed not to select any name that has already been taken (those on the board).

With younger students (or those who do not read and write), prepare individual name cards beforehand. Approach each child and offer a choice from two or three cards. Place the cards in front of the student, pointing to the corresponding name as you pronounce it. For example, *Do you want to be Hans, Georg or Heinrich?* Repeat the three names several times, pointing to the card each time until the child selects one of the cards. Keep the pace fairly brisk. Some children will say the name they want, but most will just point or take the card. If a child says s/he doesn't want any of them, try a different three names. If you still get a refusal, move on, saying you'll be back or offer to choose for him/her. This strategy usually moves the child to a quick decision.

Last Names (For Learners Beyond Third Grade)

Last names provide an opportunity to practice polite forms and extend the opportunity to learn names and titles. For languages that change verb forms for second person (you) according to the relationship between speakers, the class can address each other with last names on days they are practicing formal verb forms and with first names for informal days. Designate one or the other for a minimum of two weeks.

An alternative to providing a list of common last names in the target language is to have students pick a word that is pleasing to them and use this vocabulary word as a last name. Students choose their favorite things, such as sun, beach, chocolate, money, clothes. The teacher helps them translate, and these become their last names. Most names can be creatively illustrated on name cards or posters for the bulletin board.

New Addresses

Choosing where to live is excellent motivation for investigating the geography of the target language countries. Students also need a street name and house number to complete their address. Add to the fantasy by having them find pictures of their houses in magazines. You may want them to give written or oral presentations of their home towns or cities, and explain why they chose to live there.

Making Name Cards

To facilitate the learning of names, students who can write make their own name cards (even if it's their natural name, as in the case of ESL classes). Younger students' name cards are made by the teacher.

Provide felt pens and file cards, directing the students to write clearly in large print, taking up all the available space on the card. For last names of favorite things, require students to illustrate their name cards according to the meaning of the words.

Use unlined 3 x 5 or 5 x 8 cards (in different colors for different classes if you are collecting and storing them between meetings). If you wish the cards to sit tent fashion on the floor or desk, fold them the long way and write the name on each half of the tent so that it can be read from either side when the card is in place. Students write first and last names on separate cards, so that the appearance of first or last name cards signals which form of address to use on any given day.

If you have 25 or more students, you may need the names written larger than a folded card permits. In this case, students use one entire side of the card (do not fold) for the first name, the other side for the last name.

Students' real names can be written in pencil on the inside of the folded version or in tiny print on the flat version.

Storing Name Cards

At the end of the class period, **older students** place name cards in their notebooks and bring them the next time class meets. Those who forget name cards or lose them should quickly make replacements at the beginning of the period, using their own paper.

Storage somewhere in the room works best for **younger students.** Again, using cards or ink of different colors for each class makes the cards less likely to get mixed together when put away. At the close of each class, direct students to put their cards in the room somewhere, frequently changing the designated spot (under the table, in the shoe box, etc.). A variety of places presents opportunities for learning or reviewing words. The teacher can also designate different places for different groups, for example, *Red socks, put your name cards on the green rug; white socks, on the armchair.* The teacher or an assigned student can then gather and put them in a standard storage place.

In elementary situations where the teacher has a room and children travel to the language class, the teacher places cards on chairs or desks prior to each meeting, using a different seating arrangement each time. The two boys/two girls pattern works well.

Creating a Stress-Free Environment

Ask for Volunteer and Group Responses

Language and ego are inseparable, and many students live in constant fear of being made to look foolish. Cognitive learning increases when self-concept increases. Put your students at ease by involving the entire group whenever possible. When fewer people are required, ask for volunteers. Students will be more willing to volunteer if you first tell them what you expect them to do and then choose a minimum of two volunteers. Openly invite them to help each other.

Correct Without Putdown

Avoid negative vocabulary and directly telling learners they are wrong. When a student does an action in a manner other than directed, either describe what s/he did **without** saying, *No,* or repeat the command in a way that communicates you didn't get a correct response. For example, the teacher says, *Put the book on the chair,* and the student puts the book on the table. The teacher responds, *Put the book on the CHAIR. Put the book on the CHAIR. Put the book on the CHAIR.* With each repetition, the teacher emphasizes only the part of the response that was incorrect. A steady emphasis for the whole phrase would indicate that no part was correct.

The teacher might also tell the student what s/he actually did, *Oh, you put the book on the TABLE.* Combine the two strategies after students have had ten or more hours of instruction. Use just the first technique with rank beginners; they sometimes become confused when too many elements are added. If the student still does not respond correctly, ask for volunteers to model the correct response, or do it yourself.

When volunteers differ in responses, praise those who do it correctly, without reprimanding or pointing out those who do it incorrectly. Students are quick to figure out when they have made errors, and your lack of direct attention to their mistakes leaves their egos more intact and they will be more willing to try again. Take mental note when errors are made and re-enter the words or commands later.

Do not allow students, either through words or through actions, to put down others' efforts. Teach them to be gentle in their corrections with each other.

Don't Point

Call students by name when asking for responses or – for a more rapid and smoother pace – gesture with an open hand, palm up. Pointing is interpreted as a threatening gesture by many and should be avoided (except perhaps when disciplining).

The Beginning Speaker Is Always Right

Do not directly correct pronunciation when students begin speaking. It is tremendously ego-deflating to have one's first efforts criticized. Learners most often refine their own speech after sufficient practice. Any correction should be indirect and gentle through paraphrasing and ensuring that the student hears the correct pronunciation modeled many times.

When you must directly correct, it is much less stressful if the teacher does **not** require students to repeat the corrected response before moving on. Students also accept error correction much more readily if the focus of the correction is on the content or meaning, not on the grammatical form or pronunciation.

Help Thy Neighbor

Many of the games in this book are structured so that students work in pairs or teams. With the support of partners or teammates, stress is reduced because the risk of error is shared. If teams are small (three to five people), allow a group effort each time, but rotate the responsibility of the student who decides and says the final answer. On large teams, a total group effort is unwise because team members feel less responsibility to the group. The weaker students stay in the background and tend to rely too heavily on the best students to continually supply most of the answers. Support on large teams can be achieved by assigning partners within the team.

It is often expedient to assign partners and divide teams according to those who are seated consecutively. Doing this also avoids a popularity contest. To enable blending and cooperation of different abilities and personalities, change the seating arrangement about every two weeks.

Begin with Non-Threatening Activities

To establish rapport among members in new groups, begin with everybody-wins and nobody-loses games or those which involve chance rather than ability. Games which involve luck or little skill (rolling dice, drawing a card, guessing a number, turning an undisclosed picture) are much less threatening to the ego than those which involve acquired competence (saying or spelling a word, answering a question, especially a question to which no choice of answers is given).

Find Out More about Cooperative Learning and Self-Concept

The relationship of self-concept to learning is well documented. For more information and assistance in creating a cooperative learning environment, see *Learning Together and Alone*, and *Circles of Learning* by the Johnson brothers. Specific, usable suggestions for creating an open, caring environment can also be found in *100 Ways to Enhance Self-Concept in the Classroom* by Canfield and Wells. Their activities adapt nicely to language learning opportunities. All are listed in *Annotated Bibligraphy.*

Maintaining Student Interest

Change Activities Frequently

Brain research shows that adult learning takes place best in a 20-minute segment, and that most learning takes place at the beginning and end of the segment. With very young children or those who are not reading or writing, four or more activities may be needed to fill a half-hour period. The length and number of activities depends on the age of the learner, the complexity and variety within the activity and the interest of the material to the learner.

A successful activity can be overplayed. Listen for clues like, *Oh no, not that again!* Varying an activity only slightly will often be sufficient to maintain interest. Playing exactly the same game two sessions in a row is usually not a good idea. Introduce the vocabulary or structures in one way and choose different activities to reinforce and review.

Should Everyone Get a Turn?

If a command or activity permits only one student at a time to respond, it is seldom wise to repeat the activity enough times so that everyone can respond, unless it is a matter of a few seconds per person and the group is small. For example, only a few people should be asked to balance a broom on the palm of the hand for as long as possible, whereas everyone might participate in petting the puppy. Interest wanes unless everyone is interested in watching (and can see) the reaction or outcome with each participant. Young learners will be quick to point it out if they did not get a turn. Reassure them that the activity will be repeated another day and more will have an opportunity to try it.

Competitive games most often require a turn for everyone. Students become bored when teams are too large and their turn comes infrequently. Forming partners or small groups who act as one greatly reduces the time needed to get from group to group. Also establish time limits for responses so that everyone doesn't tire of waiting.

When Everyone Seems Confused

When there is repeated confusion in the responses of a group, it is often because too much new material has been introduced at one time. Change the activity or simplify (reduce) the elements involved. A good rule of thumb is to include some new, some fairly new and some review elements.

Multiple Props Save Time

Maintaining interest is often a simple matter of duplicating the props and materials so that more can participate at once. An example would be a tasting or smelling activity which is uninteresting to observe and needs to pass quickly. Several students can participate simultaneously by passing more than one container of the foods and scents. On the other hand, you do not want an activity to finish too quickly because the time taken to accomplish it is valuable learning time. The teacher fills the time students are passing, tasting or smelling with a continual description of the event.

Winning and Losing

Students often become discouraged if they or their team falls far behind their partners or other teams. In games where the object is to accumulate the most or the least points, cards, pictures, etc., students' interest can be maintained by announcing that the goal (to have the most or the least) will not be known until the end of the game. This usually works only if luck (not skill) determines the accumulation of points.

At the end of the game, everyone counts their points or objects to see which team or partner has the most, and who has the least. Students hold up two crossed fingers for a plus sign if they have the most or the index finger extended horizontally to indicate a minus if they have the least. Write a plus on a small scrap of paper and a minus on another. Fold the papers and mix them up behind your back, ending with one in each hand. Ask a student to select your right or left hand. If the plus is chosen, the team with the most points wins. If the minus is chosen, the team with the fewest points wins.

Another technique for keeping losing teams involved and interested is to boost the possible points for a winning play. For example, if the score is 10 to 5, announce that the next round is worth 4 points. This provides an opportunity to bridge the gap. Since it also presents the possibility of causing a losing team to fall farther behind, wait until near the end of the game to offer increased point values.

Making the Game Run Smoothly

Whose Turn Is It?

Allow larger groups to designate a team mascot (an animal or a prop) and pass it among team members to keep track of whose turn is next. In addition to acquisition of the name of the object, the passing gives everyone an excuse for a tactile encounter, including older learners who won't openly admit to wanting to hold or play with a prop. For all ages, touch enhances learning.

When the class is divided into two teams, start the mascots at points that will allow the center of interest or action to be equally distributed. For example, if the two teams are facing each other, give the mascots to people on opposite ends. If the students are in a semicircle or rows, give one mascot to the team member on the end. The opposing team's mascot goes to the person at midpoint of the semicircle or rows. These configurations are especially important when students from one team are interacting orally with the other team, because they necessitate speaking loudly to address or answer the opposing team member across the room. Students' volume is naturally low if the opponents are sitting next to or directly across from them. The other team members become disinterested if they can't hear what is happening.

Sometimes low volume means students are having trouble formulating their responses. Encourage them to seek help from partners or team members. If you assist, do it quietly within close range of the speakers so that they still have the primary responsibility for communicating.

Here are three classroom arrangements showing where to start the play. Above, a semicircle; Right, two groups facing each other; Far Right, multiple rows.

How To Divide Uneven Numbers into Teams

There are several ways to solve the problem of dividing groups evenly when there is an uneven number of students. The teacher could be someone's partner, have a group of three act as two, or give the role of scorekeeper or assistant to the extras. In relays, it is important that teams have equal numbers. To balance the competition, teams with too few people might have one member do the task twice. A less desirable solution is to assign a resting chair, requiring a student to sit out that round.

Cooperation vs. Competition (Cheering and Booing)

In team games, booing should not be permitted since a cooperative learning environment is a priority. A key element is the blend of competition and cooperation. Except for very young children, competition adds interest. Too much competition, however, puts learners under a disproportionate pressure to win and discourages risk-taking and creativity.

Cheering adds to the group spirit but may bother other classes and drown out the teacher's descriptive comments. Involved learners often need a signal (raise your hand, ring a bell, whistle, count to three) to communicate that you need their attention. When noise becomes a definite problem, issue a warning and at the same time, announce the consequence if the noise should continue. One consequence is to award excessive noise points to the opposing teams who were not involved in the noise. Another consequence is to announce no prizes will be offered at the end of the game.

Do not penalize an entire team if the disrupters are obviously only one or two people. Deal with those students individually. Individual consequences might be sitting out for a turn or a designated number of minutes, being excused last, putting away the props or being assigned to carry other students' books to the next class. It is important that students understand there will **always** be a consequence if rules are violated.

Don't Give Up Good Ideas Too Quickly

When you adapt the games in this book, or invent new ones, guard against left-brain sabotage. Sometimes one student can stifle a teacher's inspiration and a group's enthusiasm by a single negative comment. When we hear students' negativism, our overly self-critical nature leads us to conclude immediately that it was a bad idea anyway and we never should have tried it. We lose sight of the majority who wanted to play but remained silent.

Don't allow comments like, *This is dumb,* without seeking more information. Inquire sincerely, *What makes it dumb?* Students often have good insights and ideas and your genuine interest in their input builds trust and self esteem. Invite consistently negative students to give you critical reviews (written or in person) **after** the event. Solicit comments as to how they liked the game and ask for suggestions for improvement.

What To Do When It Flops

Despite the most thorough preparation, you can't guarantee students' reactions. Some activities will inevitably misfire. Don't force continuation of an activity which many students obviously don't find interesting, but don't necessarily drop it permanently either. There is always something valuable to learn from our fizzles. Rethink the event and try again, perhaps using a different group or an altered approach or structure.

Try stopping a game in mid-play and asking your students very frankly, *Why isn't this working?* Teach them to be more specific than, *This is stupid*. Their perspective and suggestions can be extremely helpful.

Learn with Scorekeeping

Although the scorekeeper marking points at the board is a privileged position, it may not be the best vantage for learning. Young children often make mistakes and arguments arise, getting in the way of the learning and enjoyment. The teacher is too often burdened with marking points or overseeing the scorekeeper when there are more important concerns for his/her attention. A further disadvantage in this scoring process is that nothing new is learned once the students know the word *point* and can count to 20 or 30. When points for opposing teams need to be recorded, there are many alternatives to tallying points on the board.

Scorekeepers could put coins, beans, paper clips, marbles, etc., in separate team containers. The teacher utilizes this vocabulary each time players score. *Add a bean to the Tiger cup* or *Put a marble in the Lion cup.* At the end of the game, the group counts aloud the score as the scorekeeper removes the objects one by one from the containers. (With the board method of scorekeeping, there is no realistic need for counting practice because everyone has a visual record on the board.) Start the counting at 30 or wherever students need to begin practice.

If students can move about the room easily, each student places his/her own point in the container as the point is made. If score is kept on the board, have the beginning score be 75 or any number the class needs to practice. Each point-maker erases the previous score and announces the new score as s/he records it on the board. Allow other team members to help, but the teacher should require that the team member announce the correct number in order to earn the point.

Sometimes cards or pictures involved in the game are awarded with a correct play. No other scorekeeping device is needed. Each team counts the accumulation at the end of the game as previously described.

Be Prepared

In selecting an activity or game, choose something that appeals to you and walk through the steps you need to take until you are familiar with the procedure. If the teacher doesn't find the material stimulating or appears hesitant and unsure, students won't be enthusiastic either and learning will be minimal.

In games like charades or verb chants which involve creativity or choreography, students need lots of examples to help their creative juices flow. Spend time planning an enthusiastic introduction which motivates and includes lots of examples.

Decide beforehand how to phrase the target vocabulary and try to use the same structures in future applications. Will you say, for example, *How are you?* or *How are you doing?* Do you tell the dog to *go get the ball, retrieve the ball* or *fetch the ball?* Is it a *trash can*, a *garbage can* or a *wastebasket* in the room? Add such variations later when students have acquired the forms originally introduced.

Making More Learning Mileage

The Importance of What's Happening

Talk about what occurs when it happens, even if it interrupts the game or the lesson. A bee flying into the room has most of the students' attention anyway, so capitalize on the occurrence to teach *bee*, describing *where it flies, fear of being stung, who likes honey, how they know it isn't a wasp, how to eject it,* as long as students maintain interest and as far as their abilities allow.

Combine the Old with the New

Recombine old and new vocabulary frequently. For example, when you introduce the word *grapefruit,* have students do every action they have learned (and maybe one or two new ones) which could apply to the grapefruit. They could *smell, hit, roll, pass, hide, eat, throw, drop, put in the...* etc.

When recombining the old and new, challenge students to figure out the correct response for combinations they have never before heard. Again, give credit to those who do it right without admonishing those who do it incorrectly. Model only those commands which stump the entire class.

Include novel and amusing commands to stimulate interest and permit the students to demonstrate thorough comprehension. For example, after teaching *stand up, walk to the table* and *sit down,* you might ask them to stand or sit on the table.

Identify phrases and directions which are needed repeatedly and change them in order to extend learning. For example, team members are frequently determined by counting off numbers *(1, 2, 3, 4; 1, 2, 3, 4).* Once students can count to four, count off teams using higher numbers, letters of the alphabet, colors or animals. A commonly used phrase is *One, two, three, go!* Instead, use any three words which can be acted or pointed out. The teacher or a student might hold up three fruits and say, *Banana, cherry, apple, begin!* An alternative would be to say, *Run, sit, throw, go!,* acting each out as said.

Repeated classroom functions and directions can be ideal opportunities to extend language. Once students know the standard phrases which accompany these functions, vary the directions. When student pass in papers, change the direction *(left, right, forward, backward) or procedure (Put your papers on the red table, give them to...).* Excuse students according to colors of hair, socks, eyes, those wearing certain clothing items, or the months of their birthdays. Invite students to also direct classroom functions.

Use Prizes as Learning Tools

When prizes are included, they should always be part of the learning, not indiscriminately chosen and handed out to the winners without comment. Select the prizes to be offered with an idea of teaching the vocabulary involved in their texture, shape, form, flavor and color. They needn't always be edible or sweet. Stickers, stamps, nuts, pencils, erasers and sugarless candy are possibilities. While one small piece of candy is usually sufficient reward for a young child, older learners reject miniscule amounts. Appeal to older students and stretch the life of a small bag of candies by having winners roll a die to see how many they will be awarded.

The awards are always of great interest to the potential winners. At the beginning of the game, this is everyone. Therefore, display and describe the prizes before play starts. If students are speaking, provide choices so that winners need to use the language to receive their preferences.

Require that students use a *please* and *thank you* when receiving prizes. This is one occasion when they don't mind being forced to speak. Provide the correct model for each student to repeat after you, and soon it will come without prompting.

Games
for
Beginners
part
3

12
9
3
6
amo
amas
amat
teh
the
violet
forest
raven
When
What
Who
apple
mine • hers
our
theirs • his
in
on
up
out
subject
verb
object
FUTURE
PAST
My Name
is Steve
2
3
4
sunny
hotly
go!
TPF

Games for Beginners

Explanations of games to students should be done as much as possible in the target language. Show the students what to do as you explain. If they do not respond correctly, help them to move according to your directions.

Icebreakers

Even if you have not selected new names, as in ESL classes, the following activities are helpful in building group rapport and establishing a safe learning environment.

Sit When You Hear Your Name

This is a non-threatening way to allow everyone to hear their own new names as well as others'.

Purpose: Introduction of Names, Commands (Listening Comprehension)

Materials: None

Procedure

After names are chosen and cards are in place, ask the entire group to stand. The students' task is to sit down as soon as they hear their names. Call out names rapidly, repeating a name until the correct person sits. To avoid giving away the answer, do not look at students as their names are called until they sit down. Then an affirming nod and a *Yes André,* reassures the person. Eye contact is needed sooner, however, to help students who do not recognize their names after several repetitions. Any other action (besides sitting down) may be substituted, such as, *Clap your hands* or *Spin around when your name is called.*

Ball Toss

Throwing is popular with most students and the movement of the ball or object holds everyone's attention.

Purpose: Introduction or Review of Names, Commands (Listening Comprehension, Optional Speaking)

Materials: Foam ball and other objects which can be safely tossed

Procedure

Toss, bounce or roll a foam ball to a student, saying for example, *Catch the ball, Vivienne. Now roll it to Herman. Herman, throw the ball to Marc.* Point out the person named if the student needs help, and indicate the meaning of the command through gestures. Balls of different sizes and colors or other objects can be added or substituted. *Throw the dog to Henri, Roll the lemon to Olga, Bounce the small green ball to Manfred.* Other verbs which can be incorporated include *give, pass, drop, pick up* and *show.* Remember that the more elements (words) involved, the greater the complexity of the task. A gradual increase is best. The teacher directs movement of the object(s) to other students until all have participated at least once.

Variation One

When students are somewhat acquainted with each other, have them all conceal their name cards. Toss the ball and other objects as described above, directing students to throw (bounce, roll, give) them to someone else. When students do not recognize names, invite others to help out by indicating the correct people. The teacher continually repeats the command and name of the intended receiver until the action is completed.

Variation Two

When students are ready to speak, invite them to participate in giving the commands. Initially the teacher begins the command and students select the names. *Vivienne, roll the ball to ...* Later, learners will be able to say an entire command. Provide choices of names and verbs when students falter.

Blind Handshake

Determining identity strictly through a handshake is an interesting challenge.

Purpose: Introduction or Review of Names, Greeting Customs (Listening Comprehension, Optional Speaking)

Materials: None

Procedure

The teacher models the command, *shake hands,* with several students and then directs everyone to shake hands with students sitting near them. You may wish to stipulate with whom, such as, *the student to your left, right, in front of,* or *behind.*

Note and discuss the differences (by showing examples) in the feel of different hands—such factors as size, smoothness, moistness. (Giving comprehensible input to communicate *sweaty* could be a real challenge.)

Ask five volunteers to participate in a blind identification of handshakes. Select one of the volunteers, say Luigi, to shake hands with each of the other four. As Luigi takes the hand of each, the teacher presents them. *Luigi, this is Antonio. Shake hands with Antonio.* The teacher might hold up Antonio's hand and make a short descriptive remark, *Antonio's hand is big.* Luigi meets the other three in the same fashion. *Shake hands with...* and similar descriptive remarks are made each time.

The teacher reviews the names one last time for Luigi who is then told to close his eyes. The four others change positions and the teacher directs one of them to shake Luigi's hand. The teacher asks repeatedly, *Who is it? Is it Maria, Gina, Antonio or Sophia?* Luigi announces his guess.

Students who know each other's native language names may be tempted to use them. Ignore a native language response, maintain a positive intonation and repeat the choices, *Is it Maria, Gina, Antonio or Sophia?* Continue to repeat the choices until you get a response. The teacher instructs Luigi to open his eyes and gives congratulations if in order. In the case of an incorrect guess, avoid the word, *no.* Simply announce the name of the person with whom Luigi shook hands. *Open your eyes. It's Gina!*

Another group comes forward and one member shakes hands with the others, then attempts to guess the identity of the person in a blind handshake. To make the identifications more difficult, increase the number of people who shake the greeter's hand and choose either all females or males for each round.

A discussion and demonstration of differences in styles of handshakes and ways of greeting among different cultures is appropriate.

Variation

A similar activity challenges students to identify the backs of their classmates. Five volunteers come forward, and Pablo is selected to stand back-to-back (backs touching) with the other four, one at a time. Communicate what you want students to do by modeling and physically guiding them into the desired positions. *Pablo, this is Enrico. Stand back-to-back with Enrico. This is Juan. Now stand back-to-back with Juan. This is Maria. Stand back-to-back with Maria.* You may wish to make accompanying remarks about height, build, or broadness of shoulders. When Pablo has stood back-to-back for a few seconds with each of the four, he faces the others and hears the names one last time. Tell Pablo to turn around and close his eyes. The teacher motions one of the four to stand back-to-back with Pablo.

Without turning or looking Pablo tries to identify the person. The teacher continually reminds him of the choices of names, asking, *Who is it? Is it Enrico, Juan, Maria...* If you wish students to make longer replies, provide the choices using the words you want them to say, *It's Enrico. It's Juan. It's Maria.* If an incorrect guess is made, the teacher either gives a choice of the remaining possible people, or asks Pablo to turn and look.

Call Down

A fun, quick review of names makes a good warm-up activity.

Purpose: Review of Names, Commands (Listening Comprehension, Optional Speaking)

Materials: None

Procedure

The entire group stands and the teacher directs several students to sit down. The teacher turns away from the group and continues to call students down, perhaps with a glance or two to see if students understand the direction to sit down. After this example, face the class and direct everyone to stand again.

Two volunteers come forward and turn away from the group. They alternate calling out names of individuals without looking back at the group. After each name is called, the teacher or the student caller directs that person to sit down. *Hans, sit down. Georg, sit down.* When student callers can think of no more names, they go stand with the group and two more callers (from among those seated) come forward. When callers repeat names, the teacher responds, ... *is already seated.* Congratulations go to callers able to seat a large number of people. Challenge them to better their own scores (number of people they could remember) when the activity is repeated another day.

Variation

The entire activity could be done in reverse, asking individuals to stand as called, rather than sit. Other verb substitutions include, *Cross your legs, open your book, put your hand on your head.*

Who's Under the Blanket?

Hiding is great fun, and everyone will want a turn under the blanket.

Purpose: Review of Names With Young Children (Listening Comprehension, Optional Speaking)

Materials: Blanket (sheet or tarp, etc.), floor space

Procedure

This guessing game works best with children up to about third grade. Play the first version with preschool and kindergarten and the variation with older children. Bring out a large blanket and demonstrate the meaning of the target phrases by asking several individuals to *Get under the blanket.* Ask the class, *Who is under the blanket?* and help them supply the names of the concealed people. As each student is named, direct them to *Come out from under the blanket.* Help them to come out if they do not respond to the command.

Eight volunteers come forward. Two of them are chosen to guess those under the blanket. The names of the other six are reviewed for the guessers who are then asked to leave the room or position themselves where they cannot see the group. While they are away, one of the six remaining volunteers hides under the blanket. If the blanket is large and the children are small, two or more may get under the blanket. Everyone else changes places in the room.

The two students rejoin the group and look around to see who is missing. The teacher asks, *Who is under the blanket?* and suggests names from the entire class. The guessers take turns responding, *yes* or *no* to the teacher's questions. *Is it Manfred? No, it isn't Manfred. There's Manfred. Is it Inga? No? Where is Inga? Inga, are you under the blanket? Yes, there's Inga.* Students come out from under the blanket when they hear their names. Expect requests to repeat the activity.

Variation

For first through third grade, provide more challenge to the original version by increasing the number of students who might hide under the blanket (more than six or, perhaps, the entire class). Again, one or two are selected to hide under the blanket. The teacher supplies possible choices and the guessers respond with the names of the hiders rather than *yes* or *no*. To make it even more difficult, require that guessers stand with their backs to the group so that they cannot see the remaining students.

Speedy Delivery

An excellent waker-upper as well as name review.

Purpose: Review of Names (Reading Comprehension)

Materials: One slip of paper for each student, 2 containers to hold papers, a stop watch or clock with second hand, team mascots

Divide students into two teams on opposite sides of the room. Provide choices of team names from target vocabulary for which you have an object—stuffed animals are popular. Have each student write his/her own new name on a small piece of paper. They should not include their real names. Collect the names from each team in separate containers and direct students to conceal their regular name cards.

Procedure

The teams take turns attempting to distribute name papers to the correct people on the opposite team as quickly as possible. A clock with a second hand or stop watch is used to time each team's effort.

The containers of names are placed in the front of the room or at equal distances between the Bear and Camel teams. On a signal from the teacher, the Bears dash to the container of Camels' names. Each Bear grabs a name paper and delivers it to the appropriate Camel. The Bears return to their seats as quickly as possible. When the Bears are all seated again, the teacher stops the timer and records on the board the number of seconds the process took. Check with the Camels to see if any were given an incorrect name. For each error, add five seconds to the Bears' score.

The Camels now try to better the time and error rate of the Bears. The team with the lowest score wins.

Let the Games Begin

Learners need to hear and understand many words and phrases of a new language before they will feel comfortable speaking. In the following activities, the teacher needs to talk as much as possible, acting out the meaning with gestures and props. The students are only physically involved at first but begin to take speaking roles after ten or more hours of listening.

Pass as Fast as You Can

This game is active yet requires no movement of people. Competition is minimized because the props are the winners and losers, not the students.

Purpose: Introduction or Review of Nouns, Commands (Listening Comprehension, Optional Speaking)

Materials: Props of target vocabulary which can be easily passed from hand to hand

Procedure

Select two objects, such as a bean and a paint brush. Give one to each person on opposite ends or sides of the room. If students are in rows, establish an S path for the objects to follow. The purpose is to see which item can reach the other end of the S path the first. Instruct the students to pass the object to the next person as quickly as they can without dropping it. Each object must pass through everyone's hands on its way to the other end of the group. During this time, repeat descriptive phrases rapidly, for example: *Pass the bean. Pass the paint brush. Don't drop it. Pick it up quickly.* The teacher says the selected phrases during the entire passing.

As soon as the people on the ends receive the bean and paint brush, they stand up. The prop which arrived first is declared the fastest and the winner. Try passing the objects in the opposite directions and comparing results.

When students are able to speak, they say, *Pass the bean* or *Here is the paint brush* as they hand the objects from one to another.

Pass and Hide

A game which easily expands from very simple to complex challenges all ages.

Purpose: Introduction or Review of Nouns, Commands, "To Have" and Adverbs of Direction—Forward, Backward, Left, Right (Listening Comprehension, Optional Speaking)

Materials: Props of target vocabulary

Procedure

Instead of passing rapidly as in the previous game, students pass objects to the next person only when commanded. At some point, the students holding the items are told to hide them. Two volunteers listen but do not watch the passing, then try to guess the people who are concealing the items passed.

Different objects, such as a toy dog and a cat, are given to two students on opposite sides of the room. If the class is in rows, opposite routes—from one end of the class to the other—must be established for the cat and dog to be passed.

Before the game begins, the students practice passing the objects to the next person, going in the established directions. The teacher randomly says, *Pass the dog. Pass the cat. Pass the cat. Pass the dog.* The teacher must watch to see that students do not pass the dog when directed to pass the cat. Only one pass is made with each command. Passing continues until the dog arrives in the hands of the person who started the cat and vice versa. Then the teacher demonstrates possible places to hide the cat or dog without leaving one's chair. Invite several individuals to hide one or the other in a pocket, behind their backs or in their hands, and describe other variations students suggest.

Once the process is understood, a volunteer is selected to keep track of the movement of the cat, another for the dog. Their task is to find the people holding the cat or dog without watching the passing or hiding. To begin the game, the cat volunteer gives the cat to a person sitting on the end of one side of the class, and the dog volunteer gives the dog to the person on the end of the opposite side of the class. Both students turn away from the class and close their eyes.

The teacher directs the passing as before and at some point, after several passes, instructs the students holding the objects, *Hide the cat* and *Hide the dog.* All other students pretend to be hiding the cat or dog. Volunteers face the group for the guessing. Since they know the routes their objects followed, and with whom they began, a mental count of the number of times the teacher said to pass the objects tells the locations.

The teacher asks the cat representative, *Who has the cat?* and provides possible answers, pointing out the students as named, *Misa has the cat, Roch has the cat, Donald has the cat. Who has the cat?* In the comprehension stage, the cat volunteer may reply by pointing or with the person's name. If more advanced, the guesser responds, *Debora has the cat.* The teacher adds, *Do you have the cat, Debora? Show your hands.* Debora must produce the cat if she has it. Speakers reply, *I don't have the cat.* If Debora was not the one with the cat, the teacher directs attention to the other volunteer, *Who has the dog?* Guessing alternates between the cat and dog volunteers until the objects are found.

Variation One

For large groups, involve more students by starting three or four objects in different areas among the students. For each object, a volunteer listens to the instructions of his or her assigned object but does not watch the passing. Objects always travel along an established route. Some students may wish to try simultaneous tracking of more than one object.

Variation Two

To increase the challenge, add the words *forward* or *backward,* and *left* or *right* in the passing instructions. Students (choose one for each object in play) eventually take over the teacher's role of directing the passing.

Air, String and Back Drawing

Drawing encourages more right-brain involvement, essential for complete language development.

Purpose: Introduction or Review of Nouns (Listening Comprehension, Optional Speaking)

Procedure for Air Drawing

Materials: None

Drawing in the air with a finger can be fun for short time periods. Announce a category of words, such as fruits. Review all the fruits you have previously introduced. With one in mind, draw it in the air, using large, well-defined strokes. If students cannot guess which fruit it is, give them choices or hints (color, how or where it grows). Invite a few students to continue, drawing their selection in front of the class.

Divide the class into partners and have them do the activity with the same or other categories. One draws and the other tries to name the object being drawn. Then the two reverse roles. Remember the goal is to communicate, not to fool one's partner.

Procedure for String Drawing

Materials: Lengths of string for each student

Provide each student with a two-foot piece of string. Suggest a simple shape to form with the string on the floor or desktops, such as a tree, boat, star, circle, square, shoe. With large groups, the teacher communicates the correct shape by drawing it on the board. Smaller groups can observe the teacher's string shape. If the words are review, ask the class to suggest shapes and wait until one or more students have formed the suggested shape before you show the correct form. Acknowledge the people who are the first to do it accurately, *Yes, that's a boat, Edouard.*

Procedure for Back Drawing

Materials: Chalkboard

Students use their fingers, capped pens, or eraser end of pencils to form simple shapes or objects on the backs of partners who try to guess the items drawn.

To model the process, choose, for example, a circle, square, star and rectangle. Draw the four shapes on the board, and repeat their names several times. A volunteer stands facing the board and the teacher draws one of these shapes on the student's back. To enable the class to observe the drawing process, the teacher stands to one side and draws at arm's length. The teacher repeats the possible choices in the same order as the drawings on the board, until the learner guesses the correct shape.

Variation One

Students form pairs for back drawing when they are ready to practice using the words. One partner draws the shapes shown on the board (one at a time in random order) and the other guesses. Then they reverse roles. The teacher circulates, continually repeating the names of the shapes so that students can tune in to the correct pronunciation. Remind them that they are trying to communicate the shapes to their partners, not to fool them.

Variation Two

Increase the challenge for older learners by adding more shapes and words to draw. Name a category (clothing, transportation, animals) or provide a list of drawable vocabulary and allow students to select any item to draw. If students enjoy this activity and are learning to read and write, try "Back Writing," page 106.

Commands Plus Objects

Language is learned best in syntactic blocks, so combining verbs with objects should be done from the beginning.

Purpose: Review or Introduction of Commands, Nouns (Listening Comprehension, Optional Speaking)

Materials: Props of target vocabulary

Procedure

Select two objects of interest, an apple and an orange, for example. Have students perform several actions with each, such as *roll the apple, touch the orange, smell, throw, catch, kick, put it on your head, drop, pick up, hide, pass,* or *eat.* When the verbs are first introduced, use only three or four at a time, adding more when you see that students are able to distinguish among those already introduced. Gradually add more objects, one or two at a time, and recombine them with all of the verbs you used with the apple and orange.

Variation

When students have heard the commands dozens of times, they will be ready to direct the teacher and other classmates to manipulate the objects. Provide two-thirds of the students with objects. Use several of the same four to eight objects, or put two students in charge of one object. Have the remaining third of the students take turns giving commands to the students holding the objects. Provide several choices of what has been practiced so students can choose what to say. If a student commands, *Hide the apple,* the teacher praises those first to hide the apple so that others can observe the correct response. Those who do it incorrectly will learn best if no attention is drawn to their mistakes.

Mini-Exercisers

When students are sleepy or have been sedentary for longer than 20 minutes, movement will carry oxygen to the brain and revitalize their concentration.

Purpose: Commands of Movement (Listening Comprehension, Optional Speaking)

Materials: None

Procedure

If space permits, have all students participate. If not, ask them to participate by rows or groups. Include such commands as *stand up, sit down, walk (forward or backward), run in place, jump, kneel, turn, go to the board, bend over, point to the flag, stand on your head, touch your toes,* or any stretches and turns you wish.

Vary the movements slightly and give them in a different order each time. If the action is new, perform it with the students; if review, wait until the students start, then join in. When students are ready to speak, invite them to lead these wake-up sessions and you join in!

Variation

Materials: Background music

Accompanying music (similar to that used in aerobic classes) played in the background is a great addition. Invite your students to bring in lively tapes or records. The leader must speak up over the music so that commands can be clearly heard.

Running Allowed

Another good opportunity to learn through movement.

Purpose: Introduction or Review of Nouns, Commands (Listening Comprehension, Optional Speaking)

Materials: Props of target vocabulary

Procedure

The first version requires some space for movement. If your quarters are really cramped, see Variation Two. Place several large objects so that they can be seen (taped to the wall or placed on top of furniture) and are far enough apart to permit running from object to object. (If your space is limited, designate a slower movement.) You may also use different parts or points in the room like the door, the pencil sharpener, over the window.

Select two students, trying to match them physically if you ask them to race. The students stand in a central location, and the teacher sends them off saying, for example, *Run to the door,* or *Jump to the window.* If neither student arrives at the correct object or point, keep repeating the correct destination or tell them where they did go rather than saying, *No.* For example, you have just asked Juana and José to run to the pencil sharpener. When Juana arrives at the pencil sharpener, say, *Yes, Juana, that's the pencil sharpener!* If José is at the door, he will figure out quickly enough that this is not the pencil sharpener without any admonishment from the teacher. Learners are more willing to try again when mistakes are pointed out indirectly in this manner. After the first pair has visited several objects, another pair is chosen.

Students will soon be able to help select where to send a pair and how. In the beginning, the teacher starts out the sentence by saying, *Run to the ...* (students fill in the blank). Later they will be able to give the entire command. Repeatedly remind command-givers of the choices of verbs such as *walk, hop on one foot, jump, skip,* and places *to the board, to the window, to the elephant.* Students will probably keep score on their own, but it's not necessary to find a winner or emphasize competition, especially for beginners.

Variation One

As a review, play the activity competitively in teams. Divide the class into three teams of five to eleven people. One team is designated to keep score and give commands, if able. The other two teams compete to be first to correctly complete the commands.

Team members are matched up with opponents by counting off from one to eight (or 18 to 25, according to students' ability), so that each member has a different number. Two chairs are placed side by side in a central location. The lowest number (or any two numbers) from each team sits in a chair. They are given a command from the teacher or the scorekeeping team. If students give the command, the teacher should repeat the command so that any errors can be corrected and students will have several opportunities to hear it. Through gestures, make sure the pair understand exactly what they are to do.

On a signal both take off for the destination as quickly as possible. The score-keeping team decides as a group which player carried out the command best and/or first. The majority rules in case of disagreement. The point for the winning team is recorded on the board.

The next lowest numbers take the chairs for a different command. Play continues until all team members have attempted to complete a command. In case of uneven numbers on the teams, someone goes twice on the team with fewer players. The roles of scorekeeping and competing teams rotate each round.

Variation Two

If you have big bodies in limited space, try this version. Divide the class into two teams. A representative from each stands behind a table of objects, facing the class. The teacher or students direct the pair to interact with the objects or give any command which does not require movement from one place to another. *Point to the door, touch the radish with your nose, pick up the pencil, smell the apple, shake the dog, scratch your head, rub the table, pinch your arm, etc.* The players receive up to five commands. The point goes to the first one who does three out of five correctly. If neither student can complete the command, the teacher or a student demonstrates and it is not counted as one of the five. The scorekeeping team awards points and gives commands or shares this role with the teacher. The game continues until all players have competed behind the table.

French Style Marbles

This game is frequently a favorite of students from about fourth grade through adult.

Purpose: Introduction of Adjectives, Measurements, Adverbs of Distance (Listening Comprehension, Optional Speaking)

Materials: One marble for each student, measuring stick, bottle, flat surface suitable for rolling marbles

Procedure

This activity resembles the French game of *Pétanque* or *Boules.* Students take turns rolling marbles toward a bottle, trying to come as close as possible to the bottle without hitting it.

Place the bottle on the floor in the center of a group seated in a semicircle. If students are at desks, position the bottle in a clear space on the floor in front of the room. Establish a point eight to twelve feet away from which students roll the marbles. If possible, have an assortment of miniature, small, average, large, and giant-sized marbles of different colors. Describe and show the selection available before distributing them. As you pass out the marbles, restate the possible choices (size and color) and comment on the one selected by each student. With large groups, provide a container of marbles for each section or row and while they are selecting, hold up and describe the available choices. Include comments on some of the students' selections, for example, *I see you chose a small green marble, Toyo.*

Students take turns rolling the marble toward the bottle (from their chairs in a semicircle or from the designated spot with large groups). If you wish to create a speaking situation, have the students announce their roll, for example, *I'm rolling a big, blue marble.* If the marble touches the bottle, it is eliminated from play for that round. Hitting another player's marble is permitted and often desirable in order to gain a better position or cause elimination of the marble closest to the object (by making it touch the target).

A meter or yardstick is used to measure exact distance of marbles near the bottle. First, second and third-place winners are declared and earn the privilege of choosing a marble before anyone else for the next round. The first-place winner begins the next round.

All action is described in continuing commentary from the teacher. Phrases used may include: *It's your turn. Roll the marble. Don't touch the bottle. You rolled the marble too hard (too gently). Who is closest to the bottle? We'll have to measure the distance. S/he hit your marble! You're in first (second, third) place! You're eliminated! You won! Winners, choose a marble. First-place roller gets first choice.*

Simon Says

This old favorite adapts easily to an effective listening comprehension game. The vocabulary used and speed of delivery varies according to the group's skill level.

Purpose: Review of Commands, Body Parts, Classroom Objects, Prepositions (Listening Comprehension, Optional Speaking)

Materials: None

Procedure

Students do as the teacher commands only if the command is preceded by the phrase, *Simon says.* The teacher always models the command, whether or not preceded by *Simon says.* When participants err by doing a command not preceded by *Simon says,* they sit down or move away from the group.

To challenge older students, the teacher should, on occasion, purposely do the command incorrectly. Students must do what the teacher says rather than what the teacher does. The teacher might point to the window saying, *Simon says, Point to the door.* Those who follow the teacher's words and point to the door are correct; those who follow the action and point to the window are penalized.

It is better if the teacher does not play the role of judge. Either let students be their own judges or appoint a group of students to make the decisions. With young children and with some groups of older students, the game is more successfully played without any penalty.

This game is usually too difficult for beginners to lead because it requires advanced skill to maintain the rapid pace and varied commands necessary to challenge most participants. If possible, invite students from more advanced classes to lead the game.

Variation

To keep all participants involved, and therefore learning longer, stipulate that on the first goof, students move to an inner circle or in front of the no-mistakes-yet group. On a second mistake, they move to an outer circle, or behind the non-erring group. A third mistake requires that they sit out.

If students are at their desks or cannot form circles, grant them three or more *lives,* represented by three objects such as books, pens or pencils on their desks. With each goof, one object is removed. When a student's *lives* are exhausted, the player sits down. At the end of the game, ask, *How many made five or fewer mistakes? Raise your hand. Keep your hand up if you made four or fewer.* Continue the count to zero. You could also have them respond according to the number of *lives* they still have at the end of the game. *How many are dead? How many still have one or more lives? Keep your hand up if you have two or more lives left.* Continue the count to five.

Shoot and Score Marbles

Students exercise their marble-rolling skills, along with their powers of prediction, then tabulate and analyze the results.

Purpose: Introduction or Review of Nouns, Comparative and Superlative, Colors, Numbers (Comprehension or Speaking)

Materials: One marble for each student, 4 to 6 containers, flat surface suitable for rolling marbles

Procedure

Gather four or more sturdy containers which make sounds when hit by marbles, such as a jar, a can, a bowl, a bottle, a vase, or a glass. Similar containers may be marked or labeled with different colors, numbers or pictures to differentiate them. Line them up on the floor in front of the class. Containers should touch each other, leaving no (or little) space between.

Before the marble rolling begins, discuss which of the containers will be most often hit (easiest or most popular) and which will be the least often hit (most difficult or least popular). The students vote by a show of hands (comprehension), or name the containers (speaking) in both categories. The total votes for each container is recorded on the board.

Students all choose a marble to roll toward the targets from a designated spot eight to ten feet away. Players take turns rolling, and the teacher or a student sits behind targets and announces which one each marble hits, placing the marble in that receptacle. If the marble hits between two targets, the roller chooses in which one it should be placed. If students do not hit the target on the first try, they may either pass or continue to roll until a hit is made. After everyone has rolled, count the number of marbles in each container to determine which has the most and fewest marbles and compare actual results with the class's prerecorded speculations. To include the comparative, ask questions about the relationships of one container to another. *The jar was hit the most often and the vase, the least often. Was the vase hit more or less often than the can?*

Variation

To play competitively, assign different point values to the containers in line with your findings of which were the hardest and easiest to hit. Divide the class into two or more teams which take turns rolling as before. For a speaking situation, have students announce the container for which they are aiming, *I am aiming for the yellow vase.* Players receive the point value of any target they hit and name, and double the point value if it is the one for which they were aiming.

Ring Fling

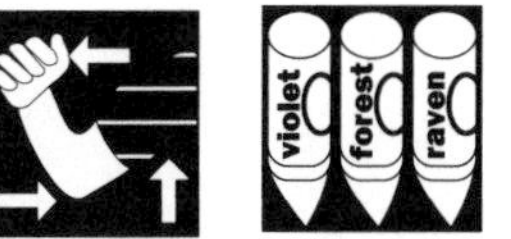

Interacting with individual objects maintains interest and enables kinesthetic learning.

Purpose: Introduction or Review of Colors, Body Parts, Prepositions, Commands (Listening Comprehension, Optional Speaking)

Materials: Plastic rings or bracelets of different colors

Procedure

Present and distribute different-colored large rings (as in ring toss games) or plastic bracelets. If there are fewer rings than students, they take turns using them in groups. Direct students to *throw, drop, pitch, hang, roll, catch* and *toss* in combination with parts of the body or things in the room. Begin by saying and doing the action with the class, then delay your actions, pointing out students who do it correctly before you do.

Possible commands include: *Red bracelets, throw them up in the air and catch them on your finger. Green rings, throw them up in the air and catch them on your thumb. Yellow bracelets, hang them on your left ear. Everybody, put your rings on your heads and jump three times.*

To collect the bracelets at the end of the activity, students might individually toss the bracelets into a basket or stand at a certain point and take turns trying to ring the neck of a bottle or miniature flag. Be sure to continually describe the play in process.

Variation

When students are ready to speak, they give commands. To emphasize using prepositions in combination with body parts, have students keep the verb constant, using either *put* or *place. Put the ring on (under, next to, in, between) your...* The teacher encourages beginning speakers by suggesting possible completions to each student giving a command, such as *Put the bracelet on your head, under your foot, between your knees.*

Pick Up Relay

This relay has lots of action and is fun for others to watch.

Purpose: Introduction or Review of Nouns, Numbers (Listening Comprehension, Optional Speaking)

Materials: 12 or more each of at least 4 common objects, 2 to 4 containers for holding objects

Procedure

Procure a dozen or more each of some easily found objects, such as marbles, corks, plastic forks, spoons, knives, plates, bottle caps, pencils, pens, or paper clips. There need not be an equal number of each object. Select four to six of these groups of items and scatter them on the floor in front of the students, mixing objects and using all available floor space. Divide students into teams of six to eight people. Their task is to gather objects as rapidly as possible.

For example, the objects scattered are knives, forks, spoons and toothpicks. Two teams of eight people stand behind a starting line. Rudi and Donna are first in line. Each receives a basket or other receptacle in which to place objects. The teacher holds one each of the objects in play and gives a starting command, *Pick up the forks and put them in your basket!* Students rush to the objects and begin picking up the forks.

The teacher holds up a fork so players can be certain of the item called. You may wish to hesitate a few seconds to give more attentive learners a slight advantage.

As the students quickly gather forks, continue to say, *Pick up the forks* several more times. Then make an abrupt change to *Pick up the spoons!* As soon as a change is given, students must pass their containers to the next teammate in line. The new player from each team picks up spoons as long as the teacher is saying, *Pick up the spoons!* The two pass their baskets to the next team members when the command changes. Young children may need a horn or other signal to ensure the change is made.

The relay ends when all team members have had a chance to participate or when no more objects remain on the floor. Students count aloud as a group (or the teacher counts if students are not yet able) the contents of each container as the last gatherer pulls the objects out one by one. The winning team is the one with the most objects.

Variation

Eventually, student leaders give the commands to pick up the different objects. This is a rewarding role for early speakers.

I Did It!

By simply adding the requirement to close eyes, practice is converted to play.

Purpose: Review of Commands, Body Parts, Prepositions (Listening Comprehension, Optional Speaking)

Materials: None

Procedure

Direct the class to close their eyes. The teacher, whose eyes are also closed, gives two or three commands which students have done previously and which can be executed without leaving their seats. *Cross your legs and put your finger in your ear. Scratch your nose and touch your left foot. Raise your thumb and put your foot on the chair,* etc. Everyone, including the teacher, follows the instructions without looking until the command, *Open your eyes!* The resulting positions and actions can be very amusing. A glance at the teacher tells them if their responses were in the ball park. Point out that often an instruction can be interpreted more than one way, so there is usually more than one right position or manner of movement.

Young children often open their eyes and upon seeing that they have correctly followed the commands, yell, *I did it!* To teach the phrase, the teacher must model it many times, pointing to correctly positioned students and supplying their words, *I did it!* Students will soon be saying it for themselves. Put students on the honor system to close their eyes. Allowing students to accuse others of looking is nonproductive. The learning is taking place whether or not students peek.

Variation

When able to speak, student volunteers give the commands to the group. The teacher should assist beginning speakers by limiting the possibilities to a few verbs at first, for example, *touch, cross* and *scratch*. Provide verb choices and suggestions for possible combinations to each command-giver. Restrict them to vocabulary previously presented. Even though students may ask you for words they have never heard, resist supplying them because most beginners cannot say words until after hearing them many times. If the words are common and appropriate, put their suggestions on your teaching agenda.

Happy Landing

Students learn vocabulary and distance relationships through tossing objects into receptacles.

Purpose: Introduction or Review of Nouns, Adverbs of Distance Near to Far, Future and Past Tenses (Listening Comprehension, Optional Speaking)

Materials: 5 to 10 non-breakable props of target vocabulary and 2 or more containers to hold props, masking tape

Procedure

In gathering props, include a mixture of review vocabulary words as well as new ones. On the floor in front of the group, place two or more large containers, such as a basket and a box. Label any two receptacles with numbers, colors or letters if you don't want to teach the names of the containers. With tape, mark two or more places on the floor, both several feet from the containers and one farther away than the other.

Young students take turns, selecting and tossing objects from close or far, according to which tape line they choose. They also choose to aim for the basket or the box, announcing their choices if they are able. The teacher continually describes choices of receptacles, distance and results as activity progresses. Objects may be retrieved each time for future play or left in the box until full.

Organize **older students** into two or more teams. Players take turns tossing the objects, scoring one or more points for those thrown successfully from the different distances. The farther the distance, the more points awarded. Establish what happens if an object bounces back out of the container (perhaps give half the point value).

Variation

If you wish a speaking element, require students to announce what and where they will toss, and from what distance. After the toss, they must state where it went. If props land in containers other than the ones for which they were aiming, players receive a lesser point value if they can state where the objects did land. Establish the pattern which you want them to say; for example, a student makes a choice from a selection of objects saying, *I choose the french fry,* moves into throwing position and announces, *I will throw the french fry into the basket from far away.* If the toss is successful, s/he says, *I threw the french fry into the basket.* Students who have difficulty speaking may receive coaching from other teammates.

The King and Queen and Their Slaves

This activity is successful with elementary children. High school or junior high students who enjoy being "on stage" also get into the spirit.

Purpose: Review of Commands, Nouns (Listening Comprehension, Optional Speaking)

Materials: A crown and a throne

Procedure

A King or Queen is chosen to sit on the throne (the teacher's chair will do) and wear a crown. In order to retain the crown and throne, the monarch must show his or her wisdom by carrying out commands given by the teacher or another student. If students are speaking, the King and Queen also describe what they are doing as they complete the command.

The monarch may continue for a limit of three commands or decline (be unable or unwilling) to do any command and choose a slave (any other student) to do it. The monarch remains on the throne until a slave is found who can carry out the action correctly. That slave then assumes the throne and crown and receives up to three commands to carry out. After three successful completions by any King or Queen, the monarch must choose a successor from the slave gallery.

Homeward Race

This game of advancing animals or people down pathways to their destinations is low in competition yet involves everyone.

Purpose: Review of Commands, Introduction or Review of Family, People, Professions, Buildings, Places, Animals and Dwellings (Listening Comprehension, Optional Speaking)

Materials: Props of people or animals, props or pictures of dwellings or destinations, paper squares for pathways

Procedure

Objects are needed to represent the people or animals, but homes or destinations (barn, cave, tree, house, boat, bakery) can be pictures. Make the pathways with small paper squares which have been cut in advance. Each pathway is four to seven squares in length and in a different color. Place animal or people objects at one end of the pathways and their corresponding homes or destinations at the other. To reduce the vocabulary involved, have several animals or people all taking a different path to the same place.

Students earn the opportunity to advance a chosen animal or person one square toward home by correctly completing a command given by the teacher, for example, *Marta, open the door. Good, now advance the cow, the horse or the sheep one square. Which do you want to get to the barn first? The cow, the horse or the sheep?* **Younger children** should be helped (preferably by another student) to do the command so that everyone is successful. **Older students** enjoy the challenge of advancing only if the command is carried out correctly without help. Dividing students into teams is unnecessary; simply call on people at random from different parts of the room. Students individually choose which playing piece to cheer for.

As time allows, the game ends after the first one is home or until second, third and fourth place are determined. After the first playing piece arrives, you could have the rain (a sprayer or container of water) arrive to sprinkle the travelers who didn't make it to shelter. Young students will be eager to play this role. Be sure to demonstrate precise instructions so that everyone does not get a shower.

Variation

When able, students give commands. In the transition from comprehension to speaking, the teacher gives a choice of two or three commands. The student leader chooses one (or a variation of one) and calls on another student to try to do it. Rotate the role of student leader.

If It Falls, It's Dead

This is a great spectators' event, even though only two people are participating for some time.

Purpose: Introduction or Review of Commands, Nouns, Death and Dying Vocabulary, Measurements, Adverbs of Distance and Direction (Listening Comprehension, Optional Speaking)

Materials: Plastic or rubber snake, frog, fly, slug, or spider. Optional: shovel, flower, student-made grave markers

Procedure

Two volunteers each select a large rubber or soft plastic animal which is somewhat villainous or distasteful, such as a snake, shark, fly or spider. The pair face each other about one yard apart, positioned so that they will have room to back up several more yards. At the direction of the teacher or other students, the two toss the animals back and forth to each other, increasing the distance between them with each toss. The object is to try to put as much distance as possible between the two players without dropping the animals. An animal instantly dies if it falls or is dropped and the toss for that animal is finished.

For example, Isumi and Kenjiro choose a spider and a fly. The teacher directs the toss, saying, *Isumi, throw the spider. Catch the spider, Kenjiro. Isumi, take two steps backward. Kenjiro, throw the fly. Catch the fly, Isumi. Kenjiro, take three steps backward.* After each toss, the player who has just thrown is directed to take one to three small steps backward. The teacher or student command-giver chooses which animal is to be tossed (alternating between spider and fly is not necessary) and how many steps the thrower moves backward (one to three). Since players are holding one animal and catching or throwing another, they must come up with ways to free their hands without putting the other animal down. If they accidentally drop it, it's declared dead. During the tossing, the teacher adds descriptive remarks like, *Will it die? Don't drop it! If it falls, it's dead! It's still alive! It's dead!*

If an animal does fall to the ground at any point, the teacher declares it dead. When the second animal dies, a meter or yardstick is brought out to determine how far each animal lived. Both are then removed to the cemetery for burial. You can have the students dramatize this as far as you choose, pretending to dig the hole, place a marker, put flowers on the grave, etc. In the imperative or third person, the teacher provides a descriptive narrative fitting the students' dramatization.

There is always sufficient interest to warrant repeating the activity. The next two volunteers select different animals to toss. Players try to achieve a distance greater than preceding students.

Young learners (under fifth grade) may have difficulty manipulating two objects but can play the game similarly, tossing one object back and forth. The teacher directs them to step backward one to three steps each time as previously described.

Frozen-to-Boiling Hide and Seek

Hide and Seek is in most students' game repertoire, so only the specific adaptations need explanation.

Purpose: Introduction or Review of Nouns, Adjectives of Temperature (Listening Comprehension, Optional Speaking)

Materials: Small props of target vocabulary

Procedure

One student is chosen to hide a vocabulary object and another to look for it. The seeker is directed to leave the room and close the door. The hider chooses a place to conceal the object (not on a person) and the seeker is asked to re-enter the room. The teacher leads the class in giving clues of *frozen, cold, lukewarm, warm, hot, boiling* or *burning,* changing the clue according to the distance the seeker is from the object. When the seeker is far away, the class chants, *frozen, frozen, frozen,* then progresses to *cold, lukewarm, etc.,* as the hiding place is approached. Any wrong movement (away from the object) produces progressive hints toward the cold end of the scale.

Introduce the meaning of the clues with gestures and perhaps ice and different temperatures of water. You will need to use fewer gradations with young children, who have not formed temperature concepts, or you must be willing to take the time to teach the concepts.

Soft-to-Loud Hide and Seek

This game allows students to hear or say difficult words many times in a fun, non-threatening activity.

Purpose: Introduction or Review of Nouns, Phrases or Other Structures (Comprehension or Speaking)

Materials: Small props of target vocabulary

Procedure

Select a vocabulary prop, which will be hidden, and ask the volunteer seeker to leave the room. Young students, who often have difficulty deciding, may need a time limit to hide the prop. When the seeker re-enters the room, the teacher or class chants the name of the hidden object, such as a vacuum cleaner. The chant begins with a soft voice when the seeker is far away, becoming progressively louder as s/he approaches the hiding place: *vacuum cleaner,vacuum cleaner, vacuum cleaner, vacuum cleaner, vacuum cleaner!* The teacher will have to do the chanting alone at first, but class members will soon chime in.

Variation One

To provide more speaking opportunity, lengthen the chant to a sentence, *Find the vacuum cleaner,* or *Where is the vacuum cleaner?* or *The vacuum cleaner is hidden.* Designate a standard phrase to exclaim when it is found, such as, *There it is!* or *You found it!*

Variation Two

A musical version of this can be made up by using any simple melody, such as, *Mary Had a Little Lamb* or *London Bridge Is Falling Down.* The seeker plays the role of a predator—a frog, for example. The object hidden is a fly or other insect. After hiding the fly, the frog enters and everyone sings softly, *The frog is looking for the fly, for the fly, for the fly. The frog is looking for the fly, for the fly,* singing more loudly as the frog gets closer and announcing, *There it is!* when found.

At Halloween, Count and Countess Dracula look for blood; at Christmas time, Santa looks for his sled or reindeer. Change the words to suit the occasion, making sure they correspond to the props, actions and rhythm of the melody.

Pass the Platter

Challenge the entire group to name and remove all the objects from the platter, rather than emphasizing individual effort. They will no doubt do well as a group, and all can share in the teacher's praise.

Purpose: Review of Nouns (Listening Comprehension, Optional Speaking)

Materials: 10 to 20 small props of target vocabulary small enough to fit on a platter

Procedure

Respecting the no-grabbing-out-of-turn rule is necessary to make this game run smoothly. It is not recommended for groups larger than 20. Students sit in a semicircle. The teacher walks from one end of the group to the other, offering the platter within reach of the students. Students try to remove the objects named as the platter passes slowly in front of them.

The teacher offers the objects to the student at one end and says, for example, *Take the apple, please.* Students may remove an item only when it is in front of them. The teacher continues on to succeeding students, repeating the request until a student removes the apple. Only one item may be touched or taken at a time by the student who is offered the platter. If Yongtae takes the potato instead, the teacher says, *That's not the apple* and/or *Put back the potato* (avoid the use of the word, *No*). Move on to the next student, returning to the command, *Take the apple.* When a full pass has been made in front of the group and the apple is still unclaimed, the teacher removes it from the platter, repeats the word several times and starts a pile of objects not claimed at the end of a full pass.

The class counts the number of items the group was able to name and tries to increase the total the next time. Set up a competition with other classes to stimulate interest.

Variation

In a speaking format, a student must name it to claim it; for example, *I'm taking the apple.* Each student gets one chance per pass to name and remove an item. When students have named all of the items they can on their own, the teacher assists by naming the remaining objects on the platter without pointing out which is which.

Change Places

Most students, especially those in high school and beyond, do not get enough opportunities to get out of their desks. Kinesthetic learning is effective for many students and vital to some. This activity has lots of action and is a favorite of all age groups.

Purpose: Review or Introduction of Nouns, Phrases or Other Structures (Listening Comprehension, Optional Speaking)

Materials: 4 to 6 large objects, flashcards or pictures

Procedure

Arrange students in a circle or semicircle. Chairs are best, but desks are manageable. Any empty chairs or desks are removed. The object of the game is to change chairs when your assigned name is called and never to be caught without a chair when the changing stops.

Place four to six objects about a foot apart in front of class (in the middle of the circle, on the chalkboard tray, or on a table in front of the class). Announce that each class member will be assigned an object and that it is important that all remember which object they are. If objects chosen are a shark, a cookie, a hat and a key, the first person (starting at one end of the semicircle or with anyone in the circle) becomes a shark, the next person a cookie, the third person a hat and the fourth a key. The teacher holds up each object, showing it to each person during the assigning, *You are a shark, you are a cookie, you are a hat, you are a key, etc.* The four items are assigned one by one until all students have a name. The naming process is part of the learning so be sure that all can see and hear.

The objects are placed in a line on the floor in front of the group. Someone volunteers to make the first call and his/her chair is eliminated, making one less chair than there are students. The volunteer stands behind the objects and, facing the group, calls out any two objects or pictures. If the student cannot say the words, s/he points out the objects with a foot and the teacher makes the call. Those players having the name of the objects called must change places to any chairs other than the ones in which they were just sitting. The caller immediately tries to sit down in one of the vacated chairs. The person who does not get a chair, and therefore is left standing, is the next caller.

When two students land on equal portions of a chair at the same time, they both become callers; don't allow them to argue it out. The teacher repeats the call during the changing, holding up or pointing to the objects so it will be clear to all what has been named.

The new caller (or same one, if s/he failed to secure a seat) announces any two items for the next change of chairs. The teacher may want to allow students to call three objects instead of two, or occasionally to allow, *Everybody change!* The more objects called, the more movement there is. Caution the students on the importance of avoiding collisions. When two or more objects are called, all must remain seated and wait until the last object is called before chair-changing can begin.

At the end, ask for a show of hands of winners—those who were never caught without a chair or were never in the calling position (with the exception of the volunteer who began).

With children younger than first grade, you need enough of the same objects or pictures so that each student can hold the item s/he is named. This serves as a constant reminder to the child, plus gives the teacher the visual clue of each child's assignment in order to monitor the movement.

Variation

After a few rounds, new words can easily be substituted by assigning new names for the various groups, for example, *Those who were whales are now snowballs*. Other structures, such as verbs, adjectives, time, weather or other expressions represented by pictures and flashcards, can be used in place of nouns.

Speedy Memory

This activity is easy to set up, passes quickly, works with all ages, and needs little introduction before play begins.

Purpose: Nouns, Verbs, Phrases or Other Structures (Listening Comprehension, Optional Speaking)

Materials: 4 to 10 large picture flashcards, chalkboard tray or floor space

Procedure

The first version has listening comprehension as the goal. For more speaking, see Variations One and Two. The activity works best with groups small enough to sit in a semicircle.

Describe and place four to ten flashcards on the chalkboard tray or on the floor in front of the group. The pictures may be of nouns or depict actions or situations. Name the cards once more as you turn them face down in place. Ask a question about the location of any card, such as *Who can find the shark?* A volunteer turns over a card and, if successful, the shark is eliminated. If incorrect, the card is returned face down and the student tries again or someone else is selected to find it.

The level of the game is advanced by using more lengthy descriptions and more pictures as well as by switching some of the pictures after turning them over. The teacher could either announce the card to be found, then switch the overturned cards, or switch them, then announce the one to be found. The latter is more difficult.

Variation One

To set up a speaking situation, do not provide a description. Instead, the teacher touches (and looks at, if necessary) one of the overturned cards asking, *Is it the jacket, the hat or the umbrella?* Give three or more possible choices. More difficult is to ask, *What is it?*, without providing choices. If students can't respond, they need to hear the choices.

Variation Two

To play competitively, divide the class into two or more teams. If teams are large, assign partners within each team for support. Members of a team of three or four all assist one other. Even though team members help each other come up with the answers, the final responsibility of describing the picture rotates among individual team members. Passing the team mascot helps keep track of whose turn it is.

To begin, two partners turn a card, and two partners from an opposing team try to describe it for a point. The less advanced will need choices from the teacher. If students are unable to name the picture, the teacher holds up the card and repeats the description several times. It is then turned back over for future play. Play continues, each team in turn. The highest scoring team wins.

Prepositions

Prepositions should be introduced early because they open up a variety of ways students can combine vocabulary and express themselves, often with minimal change.

Preposition Actions

Pave the way for preposition games with a planned presentation.

Purpose: Introduction of Prepositions, Body Parts, Nouns (Listening Comprehension, Optional Speaking)

Materials: None

Procedure

Devise appropriate hand actions to teach selected prepositions, such as the following: *on* – hands on head; *under* – hands under chin; *between* – hands between knees; *around* – finger pointed down and moved in a circular motion; *in* – fingers of one hand grasped in the other hand; *in front of* – hands with palms up in front of body; *behind* – hands behind back; *next to* – both hands thrust downward beside body.

Introduce the prepositions by modeling the actions for three or four of the prepositions, adding more as students demonstrate comprehension. The students do the action with the teacher at first, then the teacher delays the action, waiting for at least one student to do it first, praising those who do. Eventually, the teacher or a student does the action and the class responds with the appropriate preposition.

Practice prepositions by placing parts of the body in different positions or by manipulating objects, such as toy cars, which can go in, over, on, under, around and behind parts of the body or other props of nouns you wish to teach.

Preposition Pursuit

Guessing games are perfect for preposition practice.

Purpose: Prepositions, Nouns, Questions and Answers (Listening Comprehension, Optional Speaking)

Materials: 3 or more small objects, any container with front, back, top, and bottom; a towel or blanket large enough to cover container

Procedure

Students try to locate objects which are hidden in front of, behind, in, under, next to or on a toy house or other container that clearly has a front and back. Place the house on a table or on the floor in front of the group and show them three small objects. A student covers the house with a blanket or towel, and the teacher asks which of the three objects s/he wants to hide. The student selects a turkey and reaches beneath the cover to position the animal either in, on, under, next to, behind or in front of the house. The teacher asks the class, *Where is the turkey? Is the turkey (is it) behind the house? Is the turkey under the house?* or, more simply, *Behind the house? Under the house?* The teacher names all of the possible positions, utilizing prepositions practiced. If the hider is able to ask these questions, the teacher should take advantage of any silent time to repeat the questions.

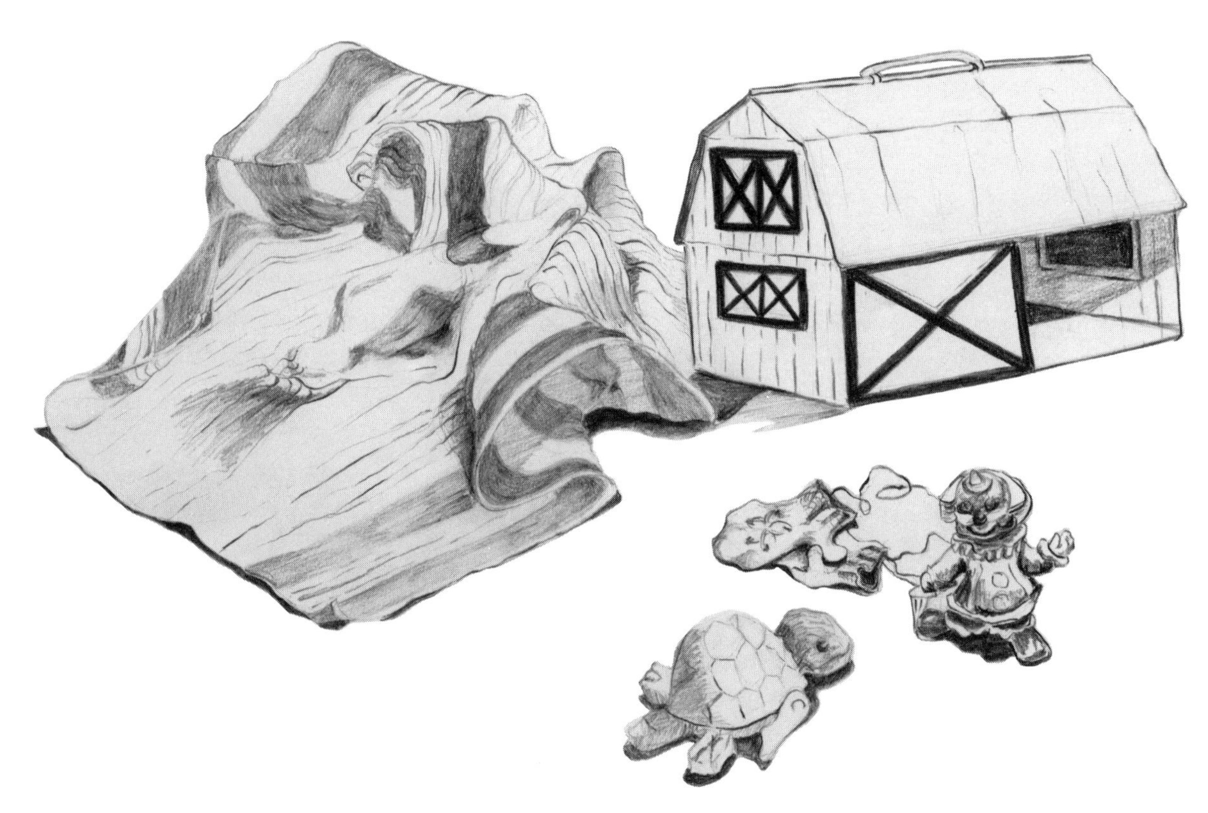

After an incorrect guess from a class member, the teacher or hider answers, *No* or *No, the turkey is not behind the house,* until the location is correctly guessed. (Use of the word *No* here is desirable to complement the negative formation. The ego is not so vulnerable because a guess is based more on chance than skill.) The blanket is removed to verify a correct guess. The successful guesser hides the same or another object, and the game continues with questions directed to those who have not yet had a chance to participate.

Variation One

To elicit a more complete response from students who can speak, hide **two** objects, such as a cat and a dog. The teacher begins by hiding a cat and a dog under the blanket in different positions in relation to the house. Divide students into partners and have them each state half of the guess. Partner A says, *The cat is behind the house;* Partner B completes the guess, *and the dog is on the house.* After incorrect guesses, the teacher says whether one or both animals were wrong, but does not indicate which one in the case of one correct answer. This information tells the next guessers whether to use part of the last pair's answer. Students may make notes, but limit the time they take to come up with guesses. The partners who finally arrive at the exact location of both animals hide the objects for the next round. The guessing resumes where it left off in the preceding round.

Variation Two

To play either version competitively, divide the class into teams of four or five. One team hides the object(s) and the other teams take turns guessing the location(s). The hiding team members take turns responding to guesses and scoring points. In the first version, one point is awarded to the hiding team for each wrong guess. If two animals are hidden, award one or two points, according to whether the guess is partially or all wrong. When all groups have had an opportunity to hide the animals, the scores are compared and a winner declared.

Command Performances

When students have spent some time in the listening stage, they will start to use the commands and eventually acquire a large repertoire. Their knowledge will grow rapidly if provided a variety of interesting ways to use commands.

Vanquish the Villain

Unsuccessful players receive a second chance to win as members of the Villain's team. Choose an outgoing student to play the role of the nasty, despicable Villain.

Purpose: Review of Commands, Nouns, Prepositions (Listening Comprehension; Optional Speaking, Reading, Writing)

Materials: 2 team mascots, a villain's hat, cape or mustache, command cards optional

Procedure

Designate one Villain and divide the class into two teams. Each team sits together in its area, and the Villain also has a designated area which will accommodate several more people. Offer a choice of stuffed animals to each team so that they may choose a name. The stuffed animals—for example, a rabbit and a hedgehog—are passed among team members to signify whose turn is next. A disguise such as a cape, hat, or mustache for the Villain adds reality and interest. The task of the Villain is to carry out the commands before the competing team.

To the Villain and one or two members of the Rabbits (working with partners reduces stress), the teacher directs a command, such as, *Find the horn and honk it three times; put a book behind the door; blow up a balloon and pop it,* or *open the window and stick your head outside!* Other Rabbits may help with gestures or with verbal assistance, but only in the target language.

The designated Rabbit partners and the Villain compete to be the first to perform the task successfully. If the command involves movement from one point to another, the Villain and Rabbits should start from the same point. If the Villain is successful, the Rabbit partners become Villains and join the Villain in his/her camp or territory. If the Rabbits are successful in completing the task first, the play passes to the Hedgehogs. The play also passes when neither the Villain nor the Rabbits can complete the task and when there is a tie.

The same procedure is followed when the Hedgehogs receive a command from the teacher. As soon as the Villain captures any Rabbits or Hedgehogs, they become villains and one assists in performing the next command. The initial Villain may remain in charge, with the role of the assistant villain rotating among the newly captured Hedgehogs or Rabbits. Others on the Villain's team may assist in gestures or in the target language.

The game is over when the Rabbits and Hedgehogs have all become villains. If time is up before that happens, proclaim the winning team the one with the most members. The villains win if their number exceeds the remaining Hedgehogs and Rabbits put together.

Variation

To add more speaking, the students invent and give commands to the opposing team. The commands could be prepared by students in advance and written on cards or slips of paper. Students take turns drawing commands to give to their opponents.

Complete the Command

This activity is ideal for encouraging beginning speakers and can be easily expanded to challenge the more advanced.

Purpose: Review of Commands, Nouns, Prepositions (Speaking, Optional Reading, Writing)

Materials: Props of target vocabulary, written command cards optional

Procedure

Teacher and students share the speaking role: the teacher begins the commands and students finish them. Divide the class into teams, for example the Belts and the Ties. Each team member takes a partner. Make an assortment of props accessible to the students to include in commands. Appoint a scorekeeper on each team.

The teacher supplies a verb, such as, *Open*, to two partners on the Belt team. The Belt partners together come up with a logical completion or ending to the command, *Open the jar*, for example. Encourage students to use the verbs, giving the entire command. If they give only a partial response, model the complete command and have them repeat it.

Two Tie partners are designated to carry out the Belt command, *Open the jar*. If correct, they earn a point for their team. Partners may help each other, but with **older learners** no help is allowed from other team members. **Young children** may not be able to refrain from helping each other, but you can still place the primary responsibility on two partners. If the action is carried out incorrectly, no point is earned.

Two Tie partners now receive a command starter, such as, *Throw*. You may wish to require that the command include a prepositional phrase. Two Belts must carry out whatever the Ties say (*Throw the cat in the hat* or *Throw the pencil in the wastebasket*, etc.). Formation of commands and actions alternate between teams in this fashion.

A point may also go to the team which composes the entire command if they did it with little or no assistance from the teacher. Awarding a point for making up the command, however, sometimes causes the students to become overly concerned with form (in order to score) at the expense of creativity. The team with the most points at the end wins.

Variation One

To focus on reading and writing, make a deck of cards with imperative verb (command) starters which have been used orally. A pair from the Belt team begins by drawing a command card from the deck, placed face down. The Belts must come up with an ending and give the command to a Tie pair within a time limit of ten to twenty seconds. If the Ties do it correctly, they earn a point. Beginning readers and younger children may need help reading the words on the cards, so do not include points for the command-makers. Continue the play, alternating between teams and rotating to different partners.

Variation Two

To extend the reading practice, make a set of completion cards (command endings) in addition to the starters. Take care to make sentences that have parts which may be interchanged without losing correct grammatical form. You could add a third stack of prepositions, adverbs or adjectives. Team representatives draw from each stack and read the combined parts to form the command for the opposing team. If the cards drawn by the Ties turns out to be an impossible combination, such as, *Open the floor,* the Belts would be awarded the point, without having to carry out a command.

Race and Place

This one is worth taking time to set up, even if you have to rearrange a crowded classroom to provide running space.

Purpose: Introduction or Review of Commands, Nouns, Prepositions, Optional Spelling (Listening Comprehension, Reading; Optional Speaking, Writing)

Materials: 12 to 20 objects, chalkboard, floor space

Procedure

Team members compete to identify or write descriptions of the objects, then put the objects in a specified place. A space for two people to run a distance of 10 to 15 feet to the chalkboard is necessary. Divide the class into two teams. Gather a set of 12 to 20 objects and divide them equally between the teams. Two sets of identical articles would ensure that names of the objects would be equal in difficulty. Separate the objects into two equal piles on the floor, one for each team.

If reading comprehension is the objective, the teacher writes the names or descriptions of the objects for each team on the board. The written words for the two teams may be mixed together or placed in separate lists. If spelling is the goal, see Variation Two.

The first two players (one from each team) stand on a marked spot or sit in chairs at equal distances (10 to 15 feet) from the board. Each is given a piece of chalk. The teacher or student instructs the players to go to the board, check off the name of the object called out, then find it in their pile and place it in, on, under, behind something or do an action with it (throw, give, hide). The teacher demonstrates the commands (or has students take a practice walk through the actions) so that both players understand. The command might be, *Go to the board, check off the word(s), find the object(s), put it (them) in the teacher's desk drawer, and return to the starting point.* The actual object which each player is to check off, find and place is not revealed until play begins.

Once both players understand what they are to do, the command is given one last time; then the teacher announces the objects each is to check off, find and place. For example, *(Command)...the mushroom and the pineapple, Go!* (Should either student move before *Go!*, both return to the starting point and the teacher names different items on the replay.) Players run to the board where one checks off the word mushroom and the other, pineapple. Then they find their items and race to place them in the teacher's desk drawer. The first to complete the process correctly and return to the starting chair wins a point for that team.

If the result is a tie, both sides receive a point. If both sides are incorrect, they may elect to try again or let other team members continue. Someone is positioned at the board to erase played words and incorrectly placed checks as well as return items incorrectly removed from the pile of objects. Play continues until all items are checked. Vary the commands slightly each time so students will be attentive to the meaning and not just perform the command by rote. For example, the students might *walk backwards* or *hop* to the board. The place where they deposit the objects could also change. The team accumulating the most points wins.

Variation One

To prepare the students to take over the command-giving, have a brainstorming session to provide them with needed vocabulary and structures.

Variation Two

To emphasize spelling, have the students write the words instead of checking them off, or have them insert missing letters into partially completed words on the board. The words to be written on the board by the next two players are announced before each play and everyone is given a minute to study before the players are chosen.

Who Wrote That?

An entertaining way to provide practice in reading and writing commands. Personal involvement motivates students to create new combinations of vocabulary.

Purpose: Review of Commands, Nouns, Prepositions, Phrases and Other Structures (Reading, Writing)

Materials: 5 containers, 2 colors of 3 x 5 file cards

Procedure

In preparation for the game, divide the class into two teams and (perhaps as homework) have each team member write on paper ten orders that they would like to see their classmates carry out. You may wish to require that they include certain verbs, nouns, prepositions or other target structures.

Students eventually try to guess the authors of the commands written by the opposing team, so caution them to seek help only from fellow team members or the teacher.

The commands may be as funny or silly as their imaginations will produce, within limits of taste. Establishing limits may take some discussion. Students will need examples from the teacher and practice composing a few as a group to get them started. Collect and correct the papers.

The next time the class meets, return the papers to the students who wrote them, and give each student one 3 x 5 card. Use a different color for each team in order to keep them separate. Each student selects five of the ten written commands and copies them on one side of the 3 x 5 card. Students cut the five sentences into separate strips and deposit one each in five different containers. Each container has one command from every student; the color signifies which team wrote them. One of the containers is selected for the first round. The others are put aside.

The first player draws a command strip in the opposing team's color and reads it aloud. A student or the teacher clarifies the meaning so that all understand. S/he then has about ten seconds to guess the author. During this time, the teacher repeats the command and also asks, *Who wrote that? Who could it be?* or makes other appropriate comments. Allow one to three guesses, depending upon the size of the group and the time available. If the guesser is correct, the author must then perform the command. If the guesser is incorrect, that student must complete the command. Points may be awarded for guessing the authors, but this game holds interest without keeping track of score. The game continues with a player from the second team drawing a strip of the other color from the container. Teams alternate until the container is empty.

Save the contents of the remaining containers for another day and repeat this activity or use the strips to play "Spin the Command Bottle".

Spin the Command Bottle

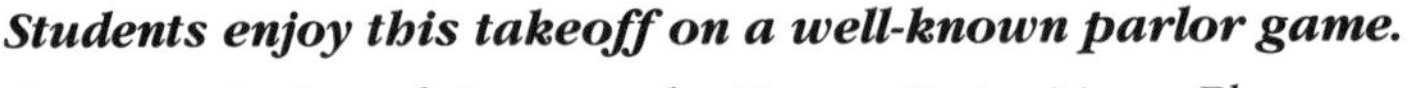

Students enjoy this takeoff on a well-known parlor game.

Purpose: Review of Commands, Nouns, Prepositions, Phrases and Other Structures (Reading, Writing)

Materials: A long-neck bottle, a container, 3 x 5 file cards or strips of notebook paper, floor space

Procedure

Students sit on the floor in a circle and take turns spinning a bottle to see who must carry out commands. See the Variation if your classroom space is insufficient to allow sitting in a circle.

To prepare for the game, students compose one or more commands which they wish to see their classmates perform and put them on cards. See the preceding activity, "Who Wrote That?" for the writing procedure. This time, secrecy is not essential, but does add an element of surprise. The orders may be on strips of 3 x 5 cards (color not important) or on strips of notebook paper.

Place a bottle and the container of command strips in the center of the circle. A volunteer draws a command and reads it aloud. The teacher makes oral corrections in the written command at this point if they have not been previously corrected. It is best if the author's name is not on the card so that no one knows who made the errors. After reading the command, the student spins the bottle and the person indicated by the bottle must carry out the command to earn the privilege of making the next spin. The teacher repeats the command several times during the completion of the command.

Younger students who are unable to carry out the commands, or who find them embarrassing, may receive help or pass. The spinner selects another person from those who volunteer to fulfill the order.

Older students will want to establish a penalty for those who are unwilling or unable to do the commands. The penalty should be something fun and harmless but slightly embarrassing, such as having to bow down to the teacher or another student or to wear a silly hat for five minutes, etc. You might have a choice of penalties and allow the spinner of the bottle to select one for the unsuccessful player. The penalties should be discussed by the class and agreed upon before play begins.

Students who successfully carry out the command, or properly pay the penalty, gain the privilege of spinning the bottle. If the bottle points to a person who has already had a turn, play automatically passes to the left (or right) to a person who has not yet participated. Respinning becomes too time-consuming. Play continues until everyone has spun the bottle and carried out a command.

Variation

If your group is too large to sit in a circle on available floor space, put half of them in the circle and assign partners who sit or stand directly behind. The bottle points to the ones in the circle. They draw the commands and enlist their partners' assistance in performing them. Upon completion, the one who drew the command spins, then the two switch places and the partner from behind sits in the circle. Play passes to the left or right after a pair has performed twice.

Pocket Games

You need pockets for the following activities. They take only a short time to make and can be used many different ways. Once students have learned the colors of the pockets, attach different numbers, letters or pictures and refer to the pockets by the new labels. You may attach the pockets to a board or they can be held individually by students who line up in front of the class.

To Make the Pocketboard

Use a large, sturdy piece of cardboard that can stand when propped against something. With different-colored sheets of construction paper or cloth (size varies according to how large your cardboard is), make pockets and attach (staple, tack, glue) to the cardboard. Pockets will need to accommodate small props, so make them at least four inches wide and five inches deep. Make one pocket in each color (8-12).

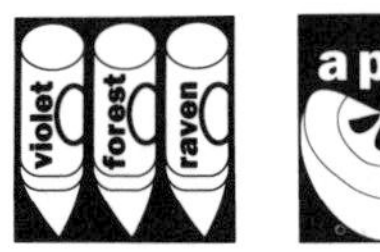

Empty or Full?

Guessing games encourage beginning speaking because the ego is less threatened when luck determines the win or loss.

Purpose: Review and Introduction of Nouns, Colors, Alphabet, Numbers, Full and Empty (Speaking)

Materials: Pocketboard, 8 to 15 props small enough to fit in pockets

Procedure

The students guess in turn whether pockets are empty or full and what items have been hidden in the full pockets. Competition can be minimized by pitting the entire class against the teacher.

Show the class eight to fifteen objects, most of which are review. The teacher hides some or all of the objects in the pockets—one per pocket, but leaving some empty. The hiding can be accomplished by turning the board or asking observers not to look. The teacher demonstrates the meaning of empty and full by showing and describing containers full of different things and some that are empty.

Starting with the first pocket, the teacher asks, *The green pocket, is it empty or full?* Let's say the green pocket has the owl hidden in it. The guesser correctly responds, *It's full.* The player earns a point for the class. Give the same player (or the next one if you have a large class) a choice of two objects which were earlier exhibited. *Is it the cow or the owl?* The response, *It's the owl,* would earn another point for the class. Remove and show the owl, reinforcing the word and the meaning, *Yes, the owl.* If a guesser says *empty* when it is full, a point goes to the teacher. That pocket's contents are to be guessed by the next student in line who receives a choice of two items, one of which is in the pocket. The class earns points when they guess correctly; the teacher earns points whenever the students are incorrect.

The teacher continues through the pockets and players in this fashion. Points are recorded on the board as earned. When all pockets have been determined empty or full and objects identified, the score is tallied to determine if the class managed to beat the teacher.

Variation One

If you don't want to teach colors, clip on pictures of nouns or flashcards of numbers or letters. You now refer to the pockets by their new identities, for example, *Is the hammer pocket empty or full?*

Variation Two

For more speaking opportunities, a student takes the hiding role of the teacher. Provide a puppet for the student so that the competition is the class against the owl or the rabbit. The puppet hides the items and responds to the questions. In the transition from comprehension to speaking, the teacher shares the speaking role, offering suggestions for choices and filling in the words as needed. Each incorrect guess would be a point for the puppet; each correct guess, a point for the class.

Which Pocket?

This is another non-threatening guessing game, but watchful students may gain some clues during the hiding process.

Purpose: Introduction and Review of Nouns, Colors, Questions and Answers (Speaking)

Materials: Pocketboard, props of target vocabulary small enough to fit in pockets, prizes optional

Procedure

The teacher or student volunteer hides an object, such as a frog, in a pocket. The class takes turns guessing the location of the frog.

The hiding can be accomplished by the turning the board around or asking observers not to look.

After the frog is hidden, the teacher says to the first guesser, *Where (In which pocket) is the frog, Marla? In the yellow pocket, the orange pocket? etc.* Marla responds, *Purple.* The teacher then says to the hider, *Marla says the frog is in the purple pocket. Is it in the purple pocket?* Expect one word guesses naming only the colors at first. Later encourage students to say, *purple pocket* or *in the purple pocket,* and eventually, *The frog is in the purple pocket.* The hider's speaking role might evolve by first responding, *No,* then, *Not the purple pocket,* and eventually, *The frog is not in the purple pocket.* The finder of the object wins the position of hiding the next object (something other than a frog unless it was found quickly and still needs to be reviewed).

Wrapped candies or stickers can be hidden in the pockets and awarded as prizes when found. If the prizes are too large for the pockets or you wish to teach other items, designate objects to correspond to the different prizes. For example, finding the nose wins a sucker.

For young children, some method of marking or eliminating the guessed pockets will be necessary, since they will not remember previous guesses and become frustrated if the item is not found fairly quickly.

Variation

Clip numbers, letter of the alphabet or pictures of nouns on the pockets if you do not want to teach colors. *Is the frog in pocket A, B or C?*

Talking Pockets

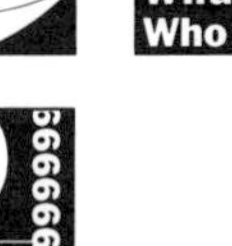

Luck plus good listening skills are required to locate the hidden prizes.

Purpose: Review of Nouns, Colors, Alphabet, Numbers, What *and* Where *Questions and Answers (Speaking)*

Materials: Pocketboard, prizes small enough to fit in pockets

Procedure

The students guess the location of prizes hidden in the letter, color, picture or number pockets of the board. Make sure your selection of prizes are words which you want to teach. Time is well spent showing and describing the prizes; interest is heightened and new vocabulary is heard in context.

The teacher turns the board and hides three different prizes, such as a sucker, a chocolate bonbon and a pretzel, in three different pockets. The board is returned and the teacher asks a student, *What do you want (would you like) and where is it?* The student answers with something like, *I want the chocolate bonbon. It's in pocket 27.* The teacher decides on appropriate structures and models them several times before beginning, then supplies possible choices during play.

If the guess is incorrect, the teacher answers either, *Sorry, the red pocket is empty* or *The bonbon is not in pocket 27, but there is something in there.* Someone else now guesses, attempting to find the same or a different prize. The students soon realize that they need to be attentive to others' guesses to help them locate the prizes. Pockets are refilled when all three prizes have been found and awarded.

Tic Tac Toes

Nine-square tic tac toes are good fillers for spare minutes. Larger grids hold interest longer and are useful for introduction or review.

Action Tic Tac Toe

***The brain is happier doing things for a reason more real than,* because the teacher said so. *Doing commands to earn plays on a game grid answers the question,* Why are we doing this?**

Purpose: Review of Commands or Questions and Answers, Introduction or Review of Alphabet or Numbers (Listening Comprehension, Optional Speaking)

Materials: Chalkboard

Procedure

Draw a tic-tac-toe grid on the board. Two students select different numbers or letters of the alphabet, say K and R (continued use of X and O is unproductive after students learn them). Players selected from the class try to place three letters in a row on the board by performing commands correctly or answering questions.

The teacher or a student leader gives a command, such as *Kick the red ball* or *Touch your left ear.* The student who carries out the command successfully earns the right to place a K or R in any square. The next successful participant places the other letter in any other square. The letters alternate without predesignating any group of students as R's or K's. If one student is unsuccessful, another student tries the same command. It is usually best to allow no more than three unsuccessful attempts; the teacher then models the correct response.

It is unnecessary to choose teams since whoever does the next command is automatically the alternate letter or team, thereby effectively de-emphasizing competition. At the end of the game, many students side with the winning letter, no matter how they played. When three K's or R's in a row are scored, a winner is declared and a new game is started. Change one or both of the letters used on the grid for succeeding rounds.

With children younger than first grade, the teacher or another student helps the volunteer carry out the task, so that all attempts are successful.

Variation

For a variation which provides more challenge, draw on the board a large grid, ten to twelve squares wide and the same number high. Divide the group into three or four teams. Each team chooses a different number, word or letter of the alphabet. Players carry out commands or answer questions to earn the right to write in the grid. The first team to get five of its symbols in a row (horizontal, vertical, or diagonal) is the winner. The commands or questions can be given by the teacher or members of an opposing team. Allow help from fellow team members if teams are small; assign partners or groups of three if teams are large.

Picture Tic Tac Toe

This versatile activity adapts easily to new or review material. By changing length and complexity of the picture descriptions, you can regulate the grammatical focus and skill level required.

Purpose: Introduction or Review of Numbers, Alphabet, Nouns, Verbs, Phrases or Other Structures (Speaking, Optional Listening Comprehension Only)

Materials: Chalkboard, 9 to 12 large picture flashcards

Procedure

Draw a grid on the board with nine to twelve squares, and write a different number or letter in each space. Remember to use letters or numbers which are appropriate to the learners' level. The students try to correctly describe pictures in order to replace the letters on the grid with their team name. The team with the most squares wins.

Show the class a group of pictures or flashcards which fit your objectives. You need as many pictures as there are squares in the grid. Review the phrases or words which describe them; see the Variation if all the words are new. Shuffle the cards and line them up on the chalkboard tray facing the board so that students cannot see them. Above each picture on the chalkboard, write one of the numbers or letters used in the grid.

Divide the class into two or more groups and have them choose team names. Allow partners or trios for support within large teams. Teams of three to five collaborate on each answer but rotate the responsibility of giving the final response.

The beginning team announces a number or letter, and the teacher turns over the corresponding card, showing it at closer range so all can see. If the students can successfully describe the picture, they replace the corresponding number or letter on the grid with the team's name or symbol. **The position of the letters on the grid does not matter; only the total number of squares claimed counts.** The described card is removed from play and the same players are entitled to a second turn, with a limit of two turns. If students are unsuccessful, the teacher gives the correct description and returns the picture to its original position facing the board. Unsuccessfully named cards must remain out of play for one turn.

The teacher announces the choices of numbers or letters remaining on the grid, and players from the next team make a selection. If they describe the choice successfully, they make an additional play. Play alternates between teams until all squares are initialed. The team with the most squares at the end of the game is the winner.

Variation One

Materials: Master list of flashcard descriptions for teacher, chalkboard, large picture flashcards

If the vocabulary involved is new, change the procedure to develop listening comprehension. Begin as described in the first two paragraphs of the preceding version. It is wise, especially for **younger learners,** to use flashcards of varying shapes so that students have clues to help them remember.

Referring to the master list, the teacher gives a description of the picture to be found, for example, *The horse is drinking water.* Each team takes turns guessing the number or letter (just one guess this time, even if successful) until the corresponding picture is found. It is important that the teacher keep repeating the description of the picture being sought, using props or actions so that all understand the meaning. The team who guesses the number of the picture initials the square. Each picture guessed incorrectly is turned back over after the teacher shows and describes it several times. The teacher does not repeat that picture description until several plays later.

In making your master list, write descriptions of the pictures on separate cards and shuffle them before play. When the pictures are determined by draw rather than teacher's choice, you are spared having to answer, *How come you gave us a hard one and theirs was easy?*

Category Tic Tac Toe

Use of objects instead of letters or numbers on the grid makes this game novel.

Purpose: Review of Nouns, Commands, Verbs, Questions and Answers, Phrases or Other Structures (Listening Comprehension, Optional Speaking)

Materials: String or tape, floor space or large table, 9 props each from 2 categories

Procedure

Form a nine-square grid with string, tape or chalk on the floor or a table. Students need to be seated in a circle or in a manner which will allow all to see the table or floor play. Individual squares on the grid must be large enough to accommodate props. Divide the class into two teams, and assign group names corresponding to the categories for which you have props. Players attempt to place three of their team's objects in a row on the grid.

You might pit fruits against vegetables, farm animals against wild animals, birds/animals, food/animals, numbers/letters, colors/shapes, clothing/household objects, or any two categories for which you have many objects. Each team's props are placed in a location that is central to the group. To earn the right to place an object on the grid, team members take turns carrying out commands, answering questions, naming objects in their category, supplying verb forms or any other learning task. Winners announce, *Three in a row!*, or something more useful than *Tic Tac Toe.* Repeat the winning phrase often during the play so that teams will learn it by the time they need to use it. It requires some visual acuity to recognize a win, since the objects all differ in form and are alike only in category.

Variation

Materials: 15 or more props each in 2 categories

To challenge older learners, increase the grid to eight to ten squares high and the same number wide. The teams compete to place five of their objects in a row, horizontally, diagonally or vertically. If props are exhausted or time runs out before either side obtains five in a row, the team which has the most objects in place is the winner.

Don't Look, Just Feel

Touching is an important part of reality, and manipulating objects helps to set them in long-term memory. In the following activities, students tune in to their abilities to distinguish form, texture and weight.

Through the Towel

Students who do not shine in normal school activities are often pleasantly surprised to discover they have refined senses of touch.

Purpose: Introduction or Review of Nouns (Speaking, Optional Listening Comprehension Only)

Materials: Basket, dishtowel, small props of target vocabulary which have similar shape, texture, and size

Procedure

The first version describes the basic process. If your group is larger than ten, follow the adaptations in the Variation. Select four or more objects which resemble each other in shape, texture and size and are small enough to hold in the hand. The older the learner, the more similar the objects need to be in order to present challenge in distinguishing among them by feel.

Place the objects in a basket or other container, naming them or asking the group to name them as you do. Cover the basket with a dishtowel. Without uncovering the objects or taking them out of the basket, grasp an object, concealing it in the middle of the towel. The basket is offered to a student who feels the lump in the towel and tries to identify the object. The teacher gives two or more possible choices, depending on the skill of the learner. One is correct. *Is it the duck, the fish, the turkey, or the lion?* Repeat the choices until the student responds. When the guess is incorrect, the teacher names the remaining objects until the guesser is down to two choices. More difficult would be to ask, *What is it?,* without giving clues. Eventually, students take the role of the teacher, making the selections and giving the choices.

A strictly comprehension format would have the teacher say, *Is it the turkey?* Student responds *No* (or nods head). *Is it the duck?* Student responds, *No,* until the teacher supplies the answer the student wishes. If the student responds, *No,* when it should be *Yes,* the teacher simply uncovers the object, saying its name.

Variation

Materials: Basket of 8 to 12 small objects, towels of different colors or patterns (1 for every 5 or 6 students)

For large groups, present a covered basket of 8 to 12 objects. They need not be as similar in size, shape and texture as in the preceding version. Describe the contents of the basket, using gestures, drawings or pictures, but do not show the actual items. Divide the class into groups of five or six students and name them according to the colors and patterns of the towels you are using.

Conceal one object in each towel and give it to the first person in each group. Instruct the students to feel but not uncover the objects. After a few seconds, signal them to pass the concealed objects to the left or right within their group. Give choices of possible answers during the passing. If an item becomes uncovered during the passing, quickly substitute another item from the basket. When everyone has handled the objects, gather all the objects and towels and stand with them in front of the room.

Hold up any one of the objects in a towel and ask all the students who handled it, *What (do you think) is in the (green) towel?* After each has answered (their answers may differ), have one of the students reveal the contents. Repeat the question-and-answer process with the other groups. It is best not to play this for prizes or points; competition makes the temptation to peek irresistible for some.

Pressing Problems

When the objects are not concealed, it is more interesting for the spectators.

Purpose: Introduction or Review of Nouns (Speaking, Optional Listening Comprehension Only)

Materials: 4 to 10 flat objects and other vocabulary objects of different shapes

Procedure

Christmas tree ornaments and cookie cutters are a good source for flat objects of different shapes. Show and describe your collection. Position a volunteer so that his/her back can be seen by the class. Select one of the objects and press it in the upper middle of the volunteer's back, asking, *What is it?* Choices are given as described in the preceding game, "Through the Towel".

Variation One

Materials: Objects small enough to be placed in the hand

Objects (not necessarily flat) may also be placed on the backs of students' hands. A student holds out a hand, palm down, and turns his/her head the other direction while the teacher places an item on the back of the extended hand. The teacher may need to steady some items with one finger. The student considers the weight and texture of the object to arrive at a guess.

Variation Two

Materials: Pair of gloves, small objects

Another method of challenging our sense of touch is to feel objects through gloved hands held overhead. Students don gloves, put their hands above their heads and try to identify objects placed in their hands. Hands over the head or behind the back prevent the player from seeing the object, but over the head is preferable because it allows others a better view of the action. Some students may choose to take on the challenge of using only one hand. Eliminate the glove element with learners younger than first grade, unless you use quite dissimilar objects.

Variation Three

For a team game, divide the class into four or five teams. The first representative faces the class and chooses one of the identification procedures previously described—on the back, on the top of the hand, or gloved hand over the head. When the student is in position, the teacher provides the object, giving choices of the possible answers. The player is allowed one response. If correct, a point is recorded for that team. If incorrect, the student sits down and a player from another team comes forward.

Weighty Problems

Make the meaning clear through dramatization rather than translation. When you think you are overplaying, you are probably doing your best work. Overplay this one.

Purpose: Introduction or Review of Nouns, Comparative and Superlative (Listening Comprehension, Writing, Optional Speaking)

Materials: Objects of varying weights, scale, chalkboard

Procedure

Show and describe a group of three heavy objects and then three light objects. Clarify the meanings by exaggerating the heaviness and lightness as you lift them. Set the light (or heavy) objects aside and draw attention to the heavy objects. Arrange them in order of *heavy, heavier* and *heaviest.* Then question your own decision and change the order, renaming the items, *heavy, heavier* and *heaviest.* Doubt sets in one more time and you rearrange the items. This time you are sure. But only for a few seconds.

In exasperation, seek the class' assistance to determine the relative weights of the objects. Students volunteer to arrange the objects from heavy to heaviest and record their guesses on the board. They write the names of each object under the appropriate column headings, *heavy, heavier* or *heaviest.* When all have recorded their guesses, the objects are weighed on a scale to determine the actual weight and relationships. The class will be interested in knowing which students successfully guessed the relative weights, but the process is actually the important part of the learning, not the results.

Objects should differ by only a few ounces if you wish to challenge older learners. The increments can be greater for younger learners.

When heavy, heavier and heaviest have been established, repeat the process with the light objects. To teach *heavier than, lighter than,* students compare two objects and make statements of what is heavier/lighter than what.

Tastes and Smells

Tastes and smells are also an important part of our sensory learning. Activities which involve eating and smelling are popular and therefore effective when students are restless, such as near the end of the year or before vacations. To cover the cost of items which everyone samples, ask students or parents to contribute the food or the money to buy them.

Identifying Edibles

The extra time spent in procuring items and setting up pays off in student interest and learning.

Purpose: Introduction or Review of Food (Edible Nouns), Adjectives Associated with Flavor and Scent (Listening Comprehension, Speaking)

Materials: Food or drinks which have distinct odors, paper plates or cups

General Procedure

Select two or more food or drink items which have distinct odors. **Young children** enjoy comparing and identifying smells and tastes which are quite different from each other. *Is it the apple or the orange?* **Older learners** want to be challenged to distinguish between similar tastes and odors. *Is it the green apple or the red apple?*

Similar foods which work well for this are apples (green and red) and pears (slightly green for easy handling); limes and lemons; oranges and tangerines; green and red grapes; yellow and black raisins; cabbage and turnips; varying brands of mineral water; different-flavored mineral waters; tap water versus mineral water; salted and unsalted butter; flour and corn tortillas; different kinds of beans; peppers of different kinds and colors; breads from different countries, and cheeses of different kinds (cow, goat and sheep milk cheeses make an interesting comparison).

Procedure for Apple-Tasting

Materials: 1 whole red apple, 1 whole green apple, 1 plate of sliced and peeled red apples, 1 plate of sliced and peeled green apples.

Distinguishing between a red and green apple is a challenging test for most students of high school age or older. Show the whole apples and ask for a volunteer who would like to try a peeled and cut sample. With apples, you can remove the peel to conceal the answer; other items require the smellers to close their eyes before tasting. Offer one of the cut samples to the volunteer saying, *Smell the apple. Is it the red apple or the green apple?* Do not expect an answer at this point, but if you get one, do not reveal whether or not it is correct. Repeat the question and possible answers while the student smells and ponders. Direct the volunteer to *Taste (eat) the apple. Is it the red apple or the green apple?* Show the answer marked on the bottom of the plate to verify the response. Repeat with other volunteers.

Procedure for Pair Work

Materials: Plates of red apple portions, plates of green apple portions, 1 toothpick per student

After modeling the tasting process with individuals, have students select partners. Distribute portions of unpeeled sliced apples. (If you peeled them, mark the plates red or green according to the color of the apple.) Each pair needs a plate of apple samples of both colors and 2 toothpicks. One of the pair closes or covers eyes and the other offers the edible with a toothpick (or guides the hand of the partner who takes it).

Establish a dialogue for students to follow: Partner A: *Close your eyes. Smell the apple. Open your mouth. Taste the apple. Is it the red apple or the green apple?* Partner B: *It's the ... apple.* Students then trade roles. The teacher circulates and repeats the dialogue in a loud voice during the entire exchange so that students can tune in to check their own pronunciations. A more controlled alternative is to have the whole class sample at the same time, and everyone repeat the appropriate lines after the teacher.

Variation

To demonstrate the close association between taste and smell, ask students to hold their noses when they taste. They may be surprised to find that it is difficult to distinguish between very different-tasting but like-textured foods (potato and turnip, radish and carrot).

Identifying Scents

Smell and memory have a strong association, yet this sense is rarely used in teaching. Here are a few ways to capitalize on the sense of smell in the classroom.

Purpose: Introduction or Review of Foods (Edible Nouns), Adjectives and Nouns Associated with Flavor and Scent, Colors (Listening Comprehension, Optional Reading, Writing)

Materials: 1 to 3 sets of felt marking pens (10 to 12 per set) with different scents

Procedure

Felt marking pens which have a different scent for each color are available in variety stores. Before class begins, list their scents or flavors on the board and randomly list another eight to keep the identification task challenging. After each scent, draw the fruit or attach a picture or object which conveys the meaning.

Present the list, then the pens to the students, and challenge them to match up the scents of the pens with those listed on the board. Explain that they will not find pens for some of the flavors listed. Distribute the pens among the students (more than one set will be necessary for groups larger than 12) and have them write down the color of each pen, then the flavor and pass to the next in line. (You may also need to list the colors on the board.)

For reading comprehension rather than writing, provide students with answer sheets which include possible answers. They match up the colors of the pens with the scents (draw a line, insert a letter or copy the word). Nonreaders make their own answer sheets by drawing the different foods and fruits next to the colors.

Require students to write their answers with a pen other than the ones in the scent test in order to preserve the odors. Establish a system for passing the pens—an established direction and a noise or other signal so students pass at the same time. During the passing, the teacher continually reminds students of the possible answers and makes appropriate comments. To help students learn the meanings, hold up the real or plastic fruits or flavor objects as you refer to them.

The correct answers are revealed after everyone has smelled all of the different pens. Remind the students that this is only the manufacturer's rendition of the odors, not necessarily **the** right answers.

Variation One

Materials: Food extracts, cotton balls, small paper cups

Food extracts used in cooking come in ten or more flavors and provide strong scents. To avoid spilling, put a dab of each on cotton balls in numbered or lettered paper cups, making yourself an answer key as you do. **For groups of more than 12,** have two or more cups for each scent so that passing will not take too long. List the possible choices on the board with illustrations of meaning and continue in one of the manners described above with the pens.

Variation Two

Materials: 2 or more perfumes, cotton balls, small paper cups

Another good odor test is distinguishing men's from women's perfumes. This is often too easy for **older learners,** so challenge them to guess the names of different perfumes. Ask them to bring in the samples. Students try to identify the different scents (on cotton balls in numbered cups again) and match them up with the names listed on the board.

Choose scents which have vocabulary you wish to teach, *True Love,* for example. Small sample bottles are often available free from department stores. See the manager and explain why you want them.

A good Valentine's Day activity is to have the class smell anonymous scents and make up names for them. On a later day, their olfactory memories could be challenged to match the perfumes with their previously assigned names.

Body Parts

Since this is a category which comes up often and is important to every learner, a variety of approaches is needed to keep the review and repetition from becoming monotonous.

Name and Touch Memory

Sense of touch enables the memory to store more information more quickly.

Purpose: Review of Body Parts (Speaking)

Materials: List of 14 or more body parts for leader

Procedure

The teacher or student leader prepares a list of body parts (about 14), one written below the other on a sheet of paper or card. The class tries to say and touch what the leader says, each time adding one more body part.

Read the first word from the list, such as *head.* Everyone (including the leader) touches and says, *head.* Then the leader says the next word, *knee,* and everyone touches the head and then the knee, saying, *head, knee.* On the third word, *nose,* the group touches and says the previously named parts, *head, knee,* and adds *nose.*

After the group gets the idea of the game, the leader touches and says only the added part each time. With each addition, the group names and touches all aforementioned parts in order, ending with the one just named by the leader. **Older learners** usually like the challenge of doing it without teacher assistance. **Younger learners** usually need the teacher to at least touch the body parts to guide them in the correct order. Continue the build-up until the list is exhausted or everybody goofs.

Variation

To add competition, the reciting can start with everyone standing. When players make mistakes, they sit down. Catching all the goofs is nearly impossible for an observer to judge, so this works best on the honor system. Those standing the longest are the winners.

Community Draw

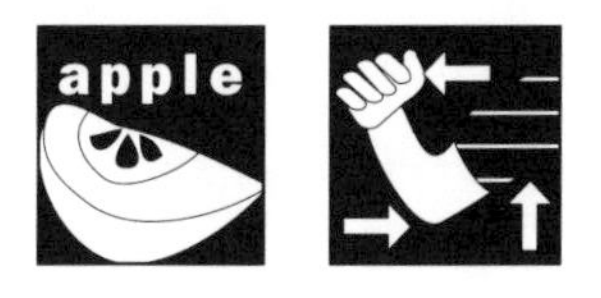

This entertaining group effort spares undeveloped artists from embarrassment.

Purpose: Body Parts, Other Nouns with Drawable Components (Listening Comprehension, Optional Speaking, Writing)

Materials: Chalkboard

Procedure

The teacher selects one or more nouns which can be divided into easily drawn parts, such as a face, body, animal, jack-o'-lantern or Christmas tree. To clarify the components, draw the chosen item on the board, naming and describing the parts as you draw. As board space allows, have two to four volunteers space themselves equally apart at the board. The teacher or a student directs them to draw one of the parts. For example, the item demonstrated was a body and the first instruction is, *Draw the head.* The teacher needs to caution the volunteers to draw only the outline and not fill in the eyes, ears, etc.

Students quickly draw the outlines of a head, then are replaced at the board by the next students in line for each row or area. The teacher may need to set a time limit for stragglers. Invite those who are not sure or begin incorrectly to check out their neighbors' drawings. Reinforce those who are drawing the correct part with an appropriate comment, such as *That's right, Bourgui, the teeth. Those are very sharp teeth.*

Increase the level of difficulty by asking for detailed items, *Draw a long, pointed, upturned nose with a wart on the end.* Do not permit drawers to change parts others have drawn.

Variation One

Materials: Sheet of unlined paper for each student

This variation allows the entire class to participate but is not recommended with children younger than second or third grade. They have trouble distinguishing what the previous people drew.

On unlined sheets of paper, students draw the part designated by the teacher or another student, then pass papers to the people next to them. Establish a direction for them to pass. You may involve the entire group in each pass or divide them into groups of four to six students who pass strictly within the group. Use actions or draw on the board to convey meaning, so that all will clearly understand the part to be drawn. Display the groups' creations, commenting on each.

Variation Two

Materials: Sheet of unlined paper per student, handout or chalkboard list of body parts

To incorporate more speaking in the passing variation, each drawer selects and tells the next student what to add to the drawing as the paper is passed. The teacher announces choices constantly, to provide ideas and models. To keep students in the target language, tell them not to draw unless the instruction was given in the target language. After the drawing is finished, the students pass the papers one final time. The person receiving the papers on the final pass labels all the parts on the picture. Provide a written list (on handout or chalkboard) of body parts to which all may refer. Use the masterpieces to decorate the bulletin boards.

Human Chain

This is probably the riskiest game in the book. At best, it will be a stupendous success; at worst, a learning experience for you.

Purpose: Body Parts (Reading, Writing)

Materials: Small slips of paper (1 or 2 per student), floor space, basket or other container for slips of paper

Procedure

On small pieces of paper, students write two parts of the body which two people could touch together without embarrassment, such as *thumb to chin,* or *elbow to back.* The class makes an amusing chain of people, hooked to each other by connecting different parts of the body. You may want boys and girls to make separate chains to avoid embarrassment or distraction.

Collect the slips of paper in a container. Two volunteers stand in a fairly large, open space. One of them draws a slip of paper and reads it aloud. The two players connect to each other by the parts indicated on the paper, such as *thumb to chin.* Whose thumb to whose chin is the players' choice. A third student draws, reads and connects with the second student. The chain continues until the whole class is connected, finger to

forehead, ankle to toe, back to head, etc., forming a twisted chain of bodies. Eliminate any obscene combinations that should come up at the time of drawing.

Variation

To play competitively between boys and girls, continue the hookups for a second round. Each student draws again and tries to make a second connection without releasing the contact from the first round. The first pair who draws a part that is impossible to join (because of the connection being held from the first time through) causes their chain to lose.

Dice Drawing

Movement and right brain involvement make an effective combination. Play is competitive but non-stressful since the dice determine the winners.

Purpose: Body Parts, Other Nouns with Drawable Components, Numbers (Listening Comprehension, Reading)

Materials: Dice, word flashcards or pictures of objects to be drawn

Procedure

Students compete in teams to complete drawings of an object. The game requires continual movement from desks or chairs to the board, so give some thought as to how this can best be accomplished in your classroom with minimal loss of learning time.

Divide students into teams of five or six and provide each team with a die. On the board write the parts of any object which can be fairly easily drawn and has at least six parts. If the object is an owl, the six divisions could be (1) head, (2) body, (3) eyes, (4) beak, (5) tail, and (6) wings. For a person, the parts could be (1) head and neck, (2) face, (3) hair, (4) trunk, (5) arms and hands, and (6) legs and feet. Parts of a Christmas tree might include (1) branches (outline), (2) trunk, (3) star on the top, (4) three balls, (5) a snowflake, and (6) two candy canes.

Each part is assigned a number, and students must roll that number on the dice to be able to draw that part. (To utilize higher numbers, make a corresponding die from a cube of sponge or wood.) Display a picture or a simple drawing of the completed object to help the drawers visualize the necessary space to allow when parts are not contiguous. To increase the vocabulary involved, have each team draw a different object.

Players and teams take turns rolling the die (instruct young children not to roll them across the room; it causes loss of time), announcing and drawing the part earned by the roll. If a player rolls a number of a part already drawn, the play passes to the next team. The teacher makes descriptive comments during the drawing. The first team to complete the object is the winner.

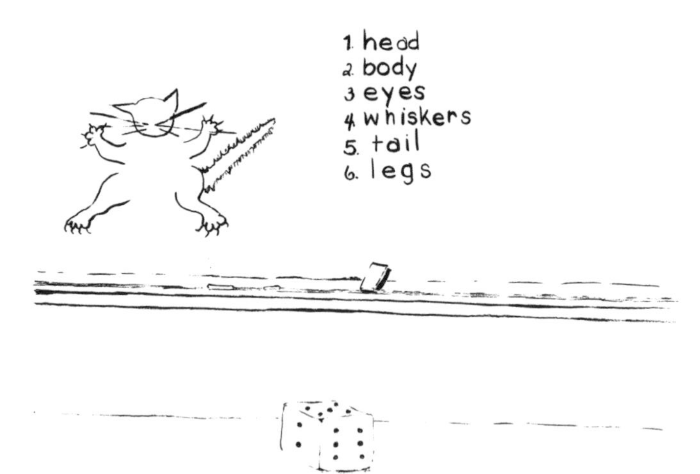

Drill Without Kill

Words need to be heard and used many times in many ways before they are acquired. The tedium of drill and repetition turns away many a language learner. The following activities suggest ways to drill and practice without killing interest.

Catch On

This game is speedy, fun practice for months, numbers, days of week, alphabet, telling time, or anything in a series or sequence. It also works well for categories such as food and colors, or for verb conjugations.

Purpose: Review of Nouns, Phrases or Other Structures in Series or Categories, Verb Conjugations, Telling Time (Speaking)
Materials: Foam ball, beach ball, or bean bag

Procedure for Days of Week or Calendar

The teacher begins by calling out the first in a series, for example dates, *Today is...* and tosses a large ball or bean bag to any student. A bean bag is easier to manage because it doesn't bounce. The catcher responds, *(Today is) June 30.* As the student tosses the bean bag back to the teacher, s/he repeats the student's correct (or corrected) answer, *Yes, today is June 30.* The teacher continues, *Tomorrow is ...* and tosses the bean bag to a student in another part of the room. That student responds, *(Tomorrow is) June 30,* and returns the bean bag to the teacher who verifies the answer, and then says, *The day after is ...* and tosses out the bean bag again. For more accomplished learners, quicken the pace by eliminating teacher's repetition of correct answers.

The tossing continues with successive days or switches to *yesterday* and the days preceding. When a student cannot respond or responds incorrectly, the teacher signals for the entire class to answer. Keep the bean bag going to different parts of the room at a quick pace and in random order to maintain interest. The bean bag is returned to the teacher after each toss to keep play from getting chaotic.

Procedure for Numbers or Time

When reviewing numbers, beginning with *one* is not always necessary or desirable. Start where it is appropriate to review and then stretch your learners. Count by twos, threes, fives, tens and backwards for variation.

To review time, designate the number of minutes later or earlier which students are to respond, for example, *15 minutes earlier.* The teacher selects a beginning time, *six o'clock,* and tosses it to a student who responds *5:45 (a quarter to six).*

Procedure for Verbs

The teacher gives either the infinitive or the pronoun, and the student responds with a pronoun and a corresponding verb form. A number of combinations are possible. The objective is stated, such as first person only, and the teacher changes the infinitive after each call. Teacher: *To write.* Student: *I write,* or require them to make a complete sentence, *I write (a letter).* Teacher: *To Eat.* Student: *I eat (an apple).* If the objective is an entire conjugation, the infinitive is announced, then the different pronouns are called as the teacher tosses out the ball. Be sure to mix up the order of pronouns after students know them in order.

Procedure for Categories

The teacher tosses the ball, calling out a category and the receivers name anything in that category. For example the teacher says, *Fruit,* and tosses the ball. The catcher says, *Lemon*, and tosses it back to the teacher who says, *Lemon*, before tossing the ball to someone else. You may have students respond in sentences, such as, *I want...*, *Give me...*, or *How much is ...?*

The category may remain the same until someone repeats something already said or no one can think of another item in that category. The last person to respond may then change the category. Keep a record of the number of items mentioned in the category, and next time challenge the class to beat the previous score.

Backward Countdown

Counting backwards helps students conceptualize individual numbers. Opposing team members race with a timer in this backward count.

Purpose: Review of Numbers (Speaking)

Materials: Digital timer with beeper

Procedure

Write ten review numbers in ascending order on the board in a horizontal line. Write the following point values in another spot: 10 seconds—5 points; 15 seconds—3 points; 20 seconds—1 point. Divide the class into two teams.

The first player comes to the board and selects a point category, according to how fast the student wants to try to count backwards. The player chooses three points, for example, so the timer is set at fifteen seconds. At a signal, the timer is started and the student begins counting in descending order, saying and indicating the numbers on the board from right to left. The student uses a pointer or a hand to touch each number as it is said.

The teacher provides a signal, such as a single clap, as errors are made. If the player is able to correct the mistake successfully, s/he may continue the backward count. Allow the player one or two attempts to correct errors. At that point, give a double clap signifying that the student must sit down. Other team members or partners could do the single clapping with advanced groups. The player receives the three points for the team if the last number is named before the beeper sounds. A representative of the opposing team follows.

You may need to increase or decrease the time limits you establish, according to the level of your group and the complexity of the numbers utilized. When students are fairly accomplished in counting backwards, advance them to counting backwards by twos, fives and tens.

Changing Digits

Number flashcards provide lots of possibilities for practice and play.

Purpose: Higher Numbers (Listening Comprehension, Optional Speaking)

Materials: Number flashcards, 10 squares of sturdy paper (preferably of different colors) per student

Procedure

Make a set of flashcards with numbers from zero to nine. Select three digits, for example, 1, 7 and 2. Demonstrate to the class the different numbers which can be formed by rearranging the position of these numbers. Possibilities are 127, 172, 217, 271, 712 and 721. Ask for volunteers to rearrange the digits (on the floor or on a chalkboard tray) as you call out the number. If you call *seven hundred twenty-one,* the student would place them in the order 721. The person doing the manipulating of the digits stands to the side so that the class can see the numbers being formed.

In order to involve the entire group, students make their own sets of numbers on pieces of sturdy paper approximately three inches square. They could use 3 x 5 cards cut in half. As much as possible, use different colors for different numbers (blue for ones, yellow for twos, etc.). The teacher calls out a number and everyone tries to form it using the cards in their deck. With large groups, have them form it first on their desks, then hold them up in the air for the teacher to see. A glance at the colors and order of colors helps the teacher spot students who are having difficulty. To verify each number called, write it on the board **after** everyone has attempted to make it. (Do not admonish those who look at neighbor's placement of cards; they need help.) Working in partners provides support and also enables the use of two decks and therefore double digits, such as 344.

Variation One

Materials: Handout of 10 or more numbers written in words and digits

For a small group activity, divide the class into groups of three or four. To one member or leader of each group, give a handout listing possible combinations of numbers, written out in words and digits (seventy-five: 75). The leader says any number from the key and the rest of the group forms it with their cards as quickly as possible. The role of the leader rotates after s/he gives four or five numbers.

Variation Two

Materials: 2 sets (0 to 9) of number flashcards

To play competitively, divide the class into two or more teams and place two chairs facing the board, about 12 feet away. A set of cards (0-9) is placed on a table or

chalkboard tray, one in front of each team. The teacher selects the same three digits from each set and demonstrates the possible combinations. Return the cards to each team's section of the chalkboard tray.

Either by teacher's choice or a lottery, runners are chosen from each team to sit in the chairs. It is important that players not be selected before the review of numbers in order to gain attention of the entire group during the review. The teacher calls one of the arrangements of numbers reviewed to the runners. Students dash to the board, arrange the cards accordingly, and run back to the chairs.

The teacher continues to call the number until the last of the two players arrives back in the starting chair. Players who change their minds may rearrange the cards, but not after they sit in their chairs. Establish a penalty for teams who call out the numbers in the first language. The penalty might be a rerun (if you are not sure which side gave away the number) or a point awarded to the opposing team's score. The point goes to the first player to arrange the number correctly and return to the starting chair. Repeat the review and play, using a new student from each team.

Increase the skill level required by omitting repeated review of the digits to be used, or increasing the possibilities (including more numbers) in the review.

Name-Calling

This chain practice bounces around the group in unpredictable order so everyone stays alert. Use short words and phrases for beginning speakers, longer ones for the more advanced.

Purpose: Review of Nouns, Numbers, Alphabet, Phrases or Other Structures (Speaking)

Materials: At least 1 large object, picture, or number/letter flashcard per student

Procedure

This activity works best if students are seated in a circle so that all face each other. Each student selects a prop, picture or number and holds it or places it so that all can see. The students' task is to be able to describe their own objects or flashcards as well as a few of those held by others.

For letter and number drills, give students flashcards with two to four letter-number combinations, such as *4-AZ, 30-WKL* or *M-107*. Expressions or other structures may be targeted, as long as they are depicted in an easily identifiable picture or flashcard or are represented by an object. The teacher describes all items in play, repeating until students know their names (expression, description or number/letter) and at least two other names.

The teacher begins by calling the name of someone's object or picture. This person responds by describing his/her object, then calling another's object. The player called responds with his/her object, then calls another, and so on. A group of students with names of fruits and vegetables might sound like this: Teacher: *Tomato*. Tomato student: *Tomato/Carrot*. Carrot student: *Carrot/Lettuce*. Lettuce student: *Lettuce/Corn*. If any student called hesitates too long, the teacher jumps in to make a call, attempting to include those people who have not been called.

The challenge is to keep the calls going at a steady clip. Players may not call back the people who have just called them. If this happens, have them make another call or the play goes back to the teacher for a restart. After all have had a few opportunities to call, students exchange objects and teach the recipients the names of the items. When everyone is comfortable with their new names, the teacher resumes play by calling a name.

Variation

Competition may be introduced by setting a time limit of three to five seconds, signified by the teacher or an official timekeeper who honks a horn or sounds a noisemaker. The goal is to move up to the first chair. (A semicircle is best for this, but the game can be played in rows, as long as the first and last chair are designated.) When a player does not call another's name within the time limit, s/he must move to the last chair in the seating arrangement. Everyone who was sitting **behind** that person moves up one chair closer to the first chair. Anyone who answers falsely, or who calls back the person who has just called them, must also move to the last chair.

The object (number, picture) stays with the chair, so all those who move take on new names. Most students are highly motivated to learn their new names after each advance and do not need prompting to ask or teach each other. Make a final check to see if all know their new names before restarting the calling.

When played with numbers or other items which progress from easy to more difficult, the most difficult one should be the first-place chair. If the person in first place manages to retain that position for more than five minutes, increase the challenge by giving that person an additional number or object. The person in first place must answer when either of the names is called.

Double Name-Calling

Once students can play "Name-Calling", they are ready for the challenge of "Double Name-Calling". The game provides an excellent strategy for combining new and review material.

Purpose: Review of Nouns, Phrases or Other Structures in Categories, Numbers, Alphabet (Speaking)

Materials: Two categories of large objects, numbers or picture flashcards

Procedure

You need an assortment of objects or flashcards which fall within two categories – one of review and one which has been recently introduced. Possible categories of nouns and expressions include clothing, food, colors, Christmas vocabulary, weather and time. You need a sufficient number of new items to allow one for every two students. There should be an equal number of review items and an additional eight to ten in reserve.

Divide students into partners and give each pair two objects, one from the category which needs to be reviewed, such as animals, and one from the newly introduced category, for example, numbers between 60 and 100. Each pair holds or places the animal and number on their desks so that all can see. No one should have duplicate numbers or animals. As in the previous game, students call each other at a steady pace, trying not to pause long enough for the horn to honk. This time, however, students have two-part names.

The teacher begins by calling an animal pair and their number, *Donkeys, 76*. The Donkeys respond with their own animal name and number, then name another animal pair, *Donkeys, 76; Snakes*. The Snakes say, *Snakes, 54; Crows* (their name and number, plus another animal). Note that the review or easier category name (animals) is said first, then the new or more difficult category name (numbers).

If the Crows are unable to say their number before an established time limit (three to five seconds) the teacher sounds a horn or noisemaker. The Crows must give up their animal to the Snakes, the ones who called them. The Crows now become a different animal, which they choose from the pile of remaining animals not in play, for example, a fish. The Fish (former Crows) are coached again on their number so that they will be better prepared next time they are called. The Snakes must now answer when either *Snakes* or *Crows* is called.

The Fish resume play by calling their name and number plus another animal pair. After all pairs have been called a few times and students are answering easily with the numbers, they exchange numbers and teach the recipients how to say them. Continual number reminders from the teacher may be necessary, but no number coaching is allowed after an animal's name has been called. As partners win or accumulate several animals, the challenge of their task increases. You could designate the ones with the most animals the winners.

Variation Two

To increase the skill level, lengthen the descriptions of objects and pictures to include verbs and adjectives, for example, *The brown donkeys bray 103; the slimy snakes. The slimy snakes hiss 1002; the noisy crows. The noisy crows caw 629; the funny fish.*

Rhythm Name-Calling

This group effort takes coordination and practice; the pride of accomplishment is great when students arrive at a steady pace with few foul-ups.

Purpose: Review of Nouns, Verb Forms – Present, Past, Future Tense, Questions and Answers (Speaking)

Materials: 1 large object or picture per student in same category. Optional: musical instrument (drum, maraca, rhythm sticks)

Procedure

This is best played with students seated or standing in a circle, but it can also be done with groups of students taking turns in front of the classroom.

Divide the group into pairs or trios. Select a category such as pastimes, sports, places or ailments. A standard descriptive phrase fitting the category is designated by the teacher. For example, with pictures of people playing sports or props of sporting equipment, everyone's phrase might begin, *We play,* and end with the name of the sport they are assigned. Give a picture or prop to each group, modeling the corresponding phrase for each. When all students have assignments, teach them how to inquire about what others play. The teacher provides a model: *We play soccer. What do you play?*

The students face each other in the circle, or ten or more students line up in the front of the room to present their sports. The beginning pair step forward and act out their sport, then look to the pair next in line to ask what they play, for example, *We play tennis. What do you play?* (Some categories may not lend to acting out, in which cases someone in the group should also show a picture to ensure communication.) The tennis players step back and the next two step forward to present their sport, *We play football. What do you play?* Direct each pair to look at the next two students as they ask, *What do you play?* The pairs continue down the line or around the circle until everyone has participated.

After all the students have presented, establish a beat to fit the length of the structure. The beat can be made by clapping or slapping the knees, or a combination of the two. Everyone learns the clapping/slapping pattern, and the teacher leads them in slapping and clapping to several examples of *We play... What do you play?* If available, a musical instrument such as drums or a maraca is a nice addition.

The pairs present as before, but this time, they try to keep in sync with the rhythm. Everyone participates in the clapping except while acting out their sport. There is no penalty for not chiming in immediately; it's all right to have a few beats of silence. The difficulty for many is to keep the words with the beat. The teacher re-establishes the rhythm when the group goes astray.

When students become confident with this version, individuals can each select a sport. The statement changes to *I play soccer. What do you play?* For practice of third person, try the Variations.

Variation One

This variation takes more coordination since the chanting goes from group to group in random order. Each group asks who is doing another action or has another item. The actions or items in play must be visible or known to all. Let's say everyone has a fruit, and the statement/question pattern is: *We have (the apple). Who has (the grapes)?* This might be chanted with two slaps on the knees for the first sentence and two claps for the second. The teacher models how to fit words of varying syllables in place of apple and grapes. The *We have ...* is said on the knee slaps and the *Who has ...* on the hand claps.

To begin, the teacher and a partner stand (or step forward) to start the group rhythm. Beginning on the knee slap beat they hold up their fruit and chant together, *We have the apple. Who has the grapes?* The teacher and partner sit (or step back in place) and the class (with the help of the teacher) responds, *They have the apple. Who has the grapes?* The pair with the grapes stand and say, in keeping with the beat, *We have the grapes. Who has the lemon?* The grapes sit as the class chants back, *They have the grapes. Who has the lemon?* It's all right if the pair called doesn't respond on the very next knee slap. The group continues to slap their knees until the fruit pair answers, *We have the* ... The group also continues the hand clap if the pair needs more than two beats to say their *Who* question.

If the students have difficulty with the group *They...* response, eliminate that part until they have practiced the *We...* several times. When responses come easily to the students, quicken the beat. After everyone has participated a few times, students exchange items for another round.

Variation Two

When students can do the *We...* version successfully, have individuals each select an item. The statement changes to *I have the banana. Who has the orange?* The class responds, *She (he) has the banana. Who has the orange?*

Among other possible phrases to set to rhythm are:

I am the fireman (we are firemen). Who is the doctor?

I have a headache. Who has a cold?

I'm eating noodle soup. Who's eating cake?

I'm at the restaurant. Who's at the grocery store?

I played tennis. Who played golf?

To utilize the past tense, students repeat the activity the next day and talk about what they *played, had, were* or *ate*. For future tense, stipulate that they talk about what they will be or do (allow fantasy here).

Bingos

This old standby is too often played in one standard way and with nouns only. Try these variations to spark interest and extend learning.

Draw a Bingo

Making the grid is part of the learning process and is an important preliminary to playing the game.

Purpose: Review of Nouns, Verbs, Negative, Phrases or Other Structures (Speaking; Optional Reading, Writing)

Materials: Chalkboard, paper, prizes

Procedure for Making the Grids

Students make individual grids with pictures and sentences, then take turns calling the items as classmates attempt to check off all squares on their papers. Choose nouns, verbs or other vocabulary which can be quickly and simply drawn by the students. The drawing does take time, but it is well spent because the teacher has an opportunity to say the vocabulary many times while students draw.

To make the nine-square grid, direct students to fold a full-size piece of notebook paper into thirds from top to bottom, and then in thirds again from side to side. The teacher announces a category, such as food, and students suggest two words from that category, for example, *milk* and *cheese.* Direct the students to draw either milk or cheese (not both) in any square on their grids. (You want students' papers to differ, so offer a choice of two items to be drawn.) The teacher draws all of the objects on the board to keep a record of the items in play. Set a time limit for drawing if necessary.

In the squares with each picture, the students write a description. The description includes the name of the item drawn and a statement which is appropriate. If the class has drawn foods, they might write either *Yum!* or *I like it* for the foods they prefer, and *Yuk!* or *I don't like it* in the squares of food they dislike.

If no words are added, be careful to avoid choosing two objects which look similar when crudely drawn, such as a pen and a knife. This is especially important with younger students. The statement of like or dislike could be symbolized with a smiling face or a frowning one.

Students continue to make suggestions of food until all nine squares are filled with pictures and accompanying words or phrases. At the end, the teacher will have 18 drawings on the board.

Procedure for Playing

To begin play, a student calls out something from his/her paper, such as, *Carrot, Yum!* (or whatever is written). This means only those having *Yum!* in the square with the carrot may mark it. Another player may choose to call *Carrot, Yuk!* The teacher quickly marks items on the board as they are called, adding a smile or frown to signify like or dislike.

Students take turns calling out items from their papers (one call per student) until someone has all nine squares marked. Winners call out a predesignated phrase, such as, *I win!* or *I have all nine!* Winning papers are checked with the record on the board and prizes are awarded.

When there is time for several rounds, players mark squares with small symbols, such as hearts, diamonds, triangles or clovers. In round one, for example, everyone who has the item called draws a heart in the lower left-hand corner. In round two they mark the squares with a triangle in the upper left corner. In round three, a diamond is drawn in the lower right corner, and in round four, a clover in the upper right corner. You could also designate numbers for different corners. Remember to include the symbol or letter when repeating a student's call. *If you have Carrot, Yuk!, mark the clover.*

After each round, students exchange papers so that vocabulary exposure will be extended. Direct them to pass papers in a designated direction, making it part of the learning. A different symbol is selected to mark in the squares. Calling resumes with the person next in line to the last caller in the previous round.

I Hate To Draw! Bingo

This version is yet another way to play Bingo and is useful for shorter time allotments since drawing is not required.

Purpose: Review of Nouns, Verbs, Negative, Alphabet, Phrases or Other Structures (Speaking; Optional Reading, Writing)

Materials: Teacher-prepared bingo sheet (duplicated for each student), prizes

Procedure for Making the Grids

Use reproduced vocabulary pictures such as those from National Textbook's *Basic Vocabulary Builder* and *Practical Vocabulary Builder,* or Addison-Wesley's *1000 Pictures For Teachers To Copy* (See *Paper Props, Flashcards* in the *Sources* section). Select any vocabulary in a single category from the sheets of blackline masters, arrange them in any order, and photocopy one for each student. As many as 16 pictures can fit on a page and still leave room for writing.

The object of the game may be to mark all squares on the grid, or to get a line vertically, horizontally or diagonally, according to how many squares are on the grid and how much time is available. Since everyone will receive identical game sheets, you must devise a way to make them differ. This is easily done by having students write in words or phrases which are appropriate to the vocabulary.

For example, students could state their preferences for food vocabulary by writing one of a choice of four statements, *I like it, I don't like it, I hate it,* or *I like it a little.* **For beginners and elementary students,** or when time is limited, reduce the choice to two statements.

You could also give students a choice of symbols, letters, phrases or numbers to draw or write at random, one to a square. Students individually make the choice of which phrase or symbol they write or draw in each square, selecting from the two to five choice provided by the teacher. For example, on the sheet of buildings, the choice of phrases given by the teacher might be: *I am in (the church, the restaurant,* etc.), *I am not in ..., I am going to the ..., I just left the ...* For less advanced students, provide choices with fewer variations, for example, different subject pronouns of the same verb, *I go to the ..., You go to the ...,* etc.

If there is time for several rounds, designate a different mark for everyone to make with different rounds. Students exchange papers after each round.

Procedure for Playing

Students take turns calling out something from their papers. Everyone who has the exact combination called marks the square, for example, *I am going to the restaurant.* The teacher makes a key for each round by writing the phrase, letter, number or symbol in each picture square as it is called.

Players who succeed in marking the number or configuration of squares needed for a win call out a predesignated phrase, such as, *I won!* The winning paper is checked against the teacher's record and a prize awarded.

Variation

To focus on the alphabet or numbers, direct students to select from among four numbers, symbols or letters for each row on the sheet. The teacher's instructions for letters would be: *In the first row of pictures, write a letter—either A B C or D—in the lower right hand corner. Use each letter once. In the second row, in the lower right hand corner of each box, write E F G or H in any order. In the third row, use I J K and L, and the fourth row use M N O P.*

The descriptions written with the pictures may be their own creations or the teacher provides a choice. Students mark their papers when they have the same letters in their pictures as the person who made the call. The sentences will not match, only the letter and word pictured in the sentence. On a food picture sheet, for example, the caller says, *I hate turnips-M.* Any student having M in the turnip picture square marks it. *I hate turnips-P* would not be a match, but *I like turnips-M* would be a match.

Card Games

Card games are an effective way to involve everyone. Cards may be teacher or student-made picture decks as well as commercial playing decks. The following hints will guide you to more productive play.

Use Commercial Decks

Commercial playing cards designed for the visually impaired have larger numbers than regular decks and work well with large groups.

For higher numbers, add zeros or any additional digit to numbers on commercial card decks. Use permanent red and black markers. Remove the face cards if these are not terms you wish to teach.

Make Your Own

Make your own decks with numbers, letters or drawings. Drawings may be used effectively both with and without written words, but the meanings of words alone are often forgotten. Students can help make the cards. Provide each student with line drawings which depict the target vocabulary or structures.

See National Textbook's *Basic Vocabulary Builder,* or Addison Wesley's *1,000 Pictures For Teachers To Copy* (listed in *Paper Props, Flashcards* in *Sources*).

Pictures from magazines and textbooks are also useful. You may have to enlarge or reduce some so that all of the pictures will be approximately the same size.

Students paste the drawings on tagboard, then cut out the individual pictures in squares or rectangles. The picture cards should all be the same size for easy handling. You can also purchase paper or plastic blank cards such as those available from Ideal School Supply Company. (See catalog section of *Sources.*)

Pointers for Playing

Play a new card game in a large group until students have learned the game and can handle the accompanying vocabulary. Then divide into small groups and provide each with a deck.

Rather than wading through the rules of a standard but unfamiliar game, ask your students how to play and have them teach you. They may know You're Lying, Crazy

Eights and Black Jack. Then check the game descriptions in this book for specific instructions on how to animate the games most effectively in the classroom.

Devise a system for quick dealing when you have large classes. Assign student helpers or pass a deck down each row so students can deal their own. In large groups, playing or discarding is done directly in front of the student. Movement to a central pile is too time-consuming.

In many of the games, the teacher can both lead and play a hand.

You're Lying!

In this game the goal is to fool your opponents. Some students learn to read eye movements to help them detect falsehoods.

Purpose: Nouns, Prepositions, Verb Forms – Present or Past Tense, Phrases or Other Structures (Speaking)

Materials: 1 regular deck for 10 or fewer players, 2 decks for 11 or more

Procedure

This game is best played in a circle. Players need to see into classmates' eyes to detect those not telling the truth about the cards they play. The object is to be the first to play out all cards dealt. If you wish to teach vocabulary other than card suits, see Variation One. For large groups, see Variation Two.

Draw the card symbols for heart, diamond, club and spade on the board or on flashcards. Spend a minute or two teaching the symbols in combination with the phrases, for example, *I play(ed) a heart* and *I too (also) play a heart.*

Distribute five to seven playing cards to each student. To expedite play with groups of more than 20, students choose partners and the two play the same hand. Players look at their cards, but do **not** allow others to see their hands.

The first player (to the left of dealer) places any card face down in front of him/her on the floor or desktop, and names the suit played, for example, *I play a heart!* The teacher repeatedly reminds students of the four possibilities, *I play(ed) a heart, I play a spade, I play...* while indicating the corresponding symbols drawn on the board or on flashcards. The next player to the left places any card face down and names the same suit, *I too play a heart.* In turn, all claim to follow suit, whether or not they actually have. The play continues in this manner with the next people in line until someone suspects that a player has no more hearts and is therefore lying. The accuser says, *You're lying!* (Students may know this game as *I doubt it!* If they are used to playing it with these words, you may want to use that phrase, instead of *You're lying!*) The accused must then show the card played.

If the accused was indeed lying and the played card was a suit different than the one named, s/he must take all cards which have been played by all players (those on the floor or desk tops) up to that point. If the accused was telling the truth, **the accuser** must take all those cards which have been played. The player who received the pile of played cards continues. S/he may change to any suit or keep it the same. The first player to run out of cards (or has the fewest when time is up) is the winner.

Variation One

Materials: 4 sets of student-made picture cards, 13 cards in each set for 10 or fewer players, 26 cards in each set for up to 20 players.

By making your own decks, this game can be adapted to teach nouns, verb infinitives, prepositions, or other phrases and structures. Refer to *Make Your Own* on page 82. Sets designed to teach prepositions and nouns, for example, might have one set of pictures with a lamp **on** the table, another set showing the lamp **behind** the table, another with the lamp **next to** the table and the fourth showing the lamp **under** the table. Make sure the cards within each set are identical in meaning.

To include more vocabulary, use different furniture or items in the four sets, such as a lamp next to a chair, a pillow on a bed, a book under the table and a cat behind the sofa. After the class practices the words describing the four sets, play as described above. The players' words change accordingly, *I plac(ed) the lamp (on, under, behind, next to) the table.*

Variation Two

For groups of 12 or more, it may be difficult to discern who yells, *You're lying*. The teacher may stipulate that only the two people on the left and right of the person who is playing the card may accuse the player of lying. The liars or false accusers receive cards only from those next to them. Another option for a penalty for the false accuser or the liar would be to receive additional cards from the dealer (perhaps the same number of cards as the number turned up by a card drawn from the deck).

Pass or Play

This is a favorite with all but the very young. The action passes quickly from player to player and can be adapted for the beginning or advanced learner.

Purpose: Introduction or Review of Numbers, Phrases or Other Structures (Listening Comprehension, Optional Speaking)

Materials: 1 deck for 10 or fewer players, 2 decks for 11 or more

Procedure

The object is to be the first to play out all cards dealt. Players are dealt an equal number of cards (five to eight) from a regular playing deck. Use two decks if there are more than 11 players. With groups of more than 20, students choose partners and the two play the same hand together. The ace plays low, serving as a one.

The first player to the left of the dealer who has an ace of any suit begins. The ace is discarded face up on the student's desk or in front of the feet on the floor. The player (or in the beginning the teacher) says, *(I have) an ace!* The next person must have a two in any suit to play. If not, the play passes to the third, fourth, or however many people are necessary to find a two. That person (or the teacher) says, *I have a two!* as the card is played. Then a three, four, five, six, seven, eight, nine, ten, jack, queen, king must be played in that order. After a king, the play returns to ace and the cycle is repeated. Only one card per turn may be played.

To direct the play, the teacher repeatedly calls out the number needed to play and also holds up fingers or flashcards to communicate the meaning. For example, when the number needed is a four, the teacher slowly passes in front of players (or uses eye contact and hand gestures if students are in rows), holding up four fingers or a flashcard and continually calling out, *four.* When capable of saying the numbers, students must say it to play it. Allow others to help. If a person says belatedly, *Oh, I have it!,* the teacher may allow play to return to that person if the card being called for has not yet been played by subsequent players. Towards the end of the game, play may pass through the entire group and no one has the consecutive card. Play then returns to the person who last discarded.

The first person to play out all cards yells, *I win!* or some other predesignated phrase. Students usually want to go for second, third, fourth place, etc. Since the game winds down rapidly, it can continue with interest until nearly everyone has played all cards.

Variation One

A version which takes less time is to allow students to play all of the cards of the same number or one or more additional cards (the next ones in the series) if they have them.

Variation Two

When students have mastered numbers to 10, add zeros to change a regular deck to higher numbers, using red and black markers. The order then becomes: Ace, 20, 30, 40, 50, 60, 70, 80, 90, 100, jack, queen, king. You could also make other increments, such as 22, 33, 44, 55, 66, 77, 88, 99, 110.

Higher or Lower?

This guessing game holds everyone's attention because each response provides a clue to the secret number.

Purpose: Review of Numbers, Comparative (Speaking)

Materials: A deck of cards or 15 to 25 numbered flashcards

Procedure

The students try to guess the number on a card held by the leader who gives the clues, *higher* or *lower*, after each guess. The student leader stands or sits in front of the group and draws a card from a playing deck or set of numbered flashcards, showing it to no one. The rest of the class tries to guess the number. After each guess, the leader indicates whether the next guess should be higher or lower. If numbered flashcards are used, tell the students the range of numbers within which they should guess.

For example, the student draws the number 44. Tell students to guess between one and fifty. The first student guesses, *32.* The teacher asks the cardholder, *Is it higher* (the teacher gestures with thumb up) *or lower* (thumb down) *than 32?* The cardholder responds, *higher than 32* (or simply, *higher).* The next student guesses a higher or lower number, according to the hint provided. The player who arrives at the exact number comes forward, draws the next card, and gives the *higher* or *lower* hints. The next person in line resumes the guessing.

Variation One

For groups of 15 or more, divide the class into two teams which take turns guessing the number. Assign partners within teams to create a more supportive atmosphere, and to involve more students at one time. To keep all attentive, randomly select partners to guess the numbers. Teams earn a point for each correct guess. The correct guessers select the next card and give the hints. Establish a higher number of points to be awarded if guessers are correct on the very first guess.

Variation Two

You can expand this idea to a game show with fabulous prizes. Students win fantasy cars, fur coats or trips to Bermuda by guessing their exact prices. Check the paper for actual prices to make the game more interesting. The total value of winnings could determine the victor in a team arrangement.

Black Jack (21)

Students will want to repeat this game, probably more than you do. Plan on 20 minutes or more.

Purpose: Review of Numbers to 21, Commands, Present Tense, Buying/Selling Vocabulary (Speaking)

Materials: 1 deck for 13 or fewer players, 2 decks for 14 or more; coins or poker chips, prizes

Procedure

The teacher deals everyone two cards. Students add up the total points of the cards dealt, hoping to be as close as possible to 21. Each numbered card is worth the face value; jack, queen and king are ten each. An ace may be used as either a one or an eleven (player's choice). If players' cards total 15 or less, they may want to be *hit* with another card by the dealer. If the cards total 18, 19, 20, or 21, players should *stay*. If players choose to risk getting closer to 21, they ask to be *hit* (receive another card from the dealer). If the total goes over 21, they are *broke* and have no chance of winning that hand.

After dealing the initial two cards, the dealer (teacher) immediately approaches players again, suggesting what they wish to say to the dealer, either, *I stay!* or *Hit me!* The dealer gives a third card to everyone who wishes to be *hit* and then a fourth and fifth if necessary. (Players who accumulate five cards without going *broke*, or over 21, automatically win or beat the dealer.)

Players are *hit* as many times as they wish, then the dealer takes two cards. The dealer shows and announces the cards to the class, who respond with the total point value. The dealer seeks the class's advice to either continue or stay. The dealer **must** take a *hit* if the total of the cards is 15 or less points. The dealer *stays* at 21 or when close to 21. All players who come closer to 21 than the dealer are paid with one coin or token of any kind. A dealer's hand totaling 19 would pay those who had 20 or 21. If the dealer goes *broke*, all those who scored 21 or under are paid.

The dealer can use poker chips, beans, foreign coins or any other token to *pay* the players (one per winner) after each round. Winners must show their cards, announce their total, and say, *Pay me, please*, to receive payment. After several rounds, the teacher sells candy or minor prizes. Present and describe items for sale and explain prices before the sales begin. (Provide a choice of prizes which vary in value.) The teacher either goes to students with a basket of goodies for sale or students come *to the store*. Transactions include the teacher's description of the items and costs and the students' statements of what they would like to buy.

After each round, students are directed to pass all cards to a certain point. Someone is assigned to gather and shuffle the decks just used so they will be ready for the next round.

Variation

For groups over 13, assign partners and/or ask for a student dealer to take over half of the class. Dealers work simultaneously but with separate decks, dealing one hand to each pair. Partners refer to *we* and *us* instead of *I* and *me*, when communicating with the dealer(s). When the two dealers deal themselves hands, one dealer precedes the other to focus the group's attention and response.

I've Got It!

This is a good game for learning new vocabulary because the same word or phrase reappears four times. If material is quite familiar, speed up the calling to maintain interest.

Purpose: Introduction or Review of Numbers, Telling Time, Nouns, Verbs, Colors, Prepositions, Phrases or Other Structures (Speaking, Optional Listening Comprehension Only)

Materials: 1 deck for dealer, plus 1 deck for 10 or fewer students, 2 decks for 11 to 20, 3 decks for more than 20

Procedure

If you wish to teach vocabulary other than numbers, see Variation Two. The object is to play out all cards dealt. Everyone receives five to seven cards. It doesn't matter if they see others' cards. The teacher or student leader places a complete deck face down in front of the group. The leader draws the first card and announces its name and color such as, *Black ace*. The two (or more) students who have it yell, *I've got it!*, and place the cards (ace of clubs and ace of spades) face up in front of them on the floor or desktops. The leader shows the card called each time (so that all know for sure what it was) but not immediately after the call, allowing time to think and for responses of *I've got it!*

Occasionally praise players who make correct plays before you show the cards, *Yes, a red nine, Joe*. If you spot someone playing an incorrect card, describe what the student has played and show the correct card again, saying its name.

The leader lays out the cards as called, face up, according to number and suit, so that questions on what has been called can be readily answered. Succeeding cards are drawn from the top of the deck and called out by the leader in the same fashion. The first player to play out all cards yells a phrase, such as, *I won!* When a card that has already been called is drawn (there are two of each color in the caller's deck), the teacher says, *Already called!* There is usually enough interest to go for second, third, and fourth places and even until everyone has played out all cards.

Variation One

Materials: Flashcards or chalkboard drawings of a heart, spade, club, and diamond

For older students, you may wish to name the suits as well as numbers—*Ace of spades!, Seven of clubs!* In large groups, it may be hard to distinguish spade from club and diamond from heart on the teacher-held card, when shown. To avoid confusion, draw large symbols of the suits on the board or flashcards and keep referring to them as needed during play. This variation is less fun for younger children, who like the action to pass more quickly.

Variation Two

Materials: 1 deck of student-made cards for the dealer and 1 deck for every 10 players

By making your own decks, this game can be adapted to teach nouns, telling time, verbs, prepositions, or phrases and other structures. For easy assembly, refer to *Make Your Own* on page 82. The basic design of your deck will resemble that of a regular playing deck, four each of 13 kinds. A deck produced to teach time, for example, would have pictures of clocks showing 13 different times, four cards of each one. (A rising and setting sun, moon and stars can indicate morning, afternoon, evening or night.)

Like the red and black of regular cards, print or draw two of the cards in each foursome on one color of paper and the other two on a different color. If two of the seven o'clock pictures were blue, the other two could be white.

After the class practices the words describing the four sets, play as described in the original version. The leader draws from a shuffled deck and calls out the time, *It is seven o'clock in the evening – blue.*

Crazy Eights

Each player has the option of playing any of three ways. Keep the action lively by establishing a time limit for poky players.

Purpose: Review of Numbers, Review or Introduction of Card Suits (Speaking, Optional Listening Comprehension)

Materials: 1 deck for dealer, plus 1 deck for 10 or fewer students, 2 decks for 11 to 20, 3 decks for more than 20

Procedure

The object of the game is to play out all cards dealt. This version is for 15 or fewer people sitting in a circle. For larger groups, see Variation Two.

Students each receive five to eight cards. Place another deck of cards face down in the center, or if the circle is large, position several decks at various points so that they will be convenient for drawing additional cards.

To begin, the dealer turns up a card from the deck in the middle and names the number and suit, saying for example, *Seven of hearts.* The student next to the dealer may play any of three ways. S/he may discard a heart which would keep the play in hearts. A second option would be to discard the same number (seven) of another suit. This changes the suit to match the card played. The seven of clubs would change the play to clubs. Finally, any eight may be played. The *crazy eight* has the power to permit change to whatever suit a player wishes, regardless of the suit showing on the eight. The player makes one of the three choices and announces the number of the card and the suit (help from the teacher or other students is freely given) upon discarding.

A player who cannot play by any of the three ways mentioned (a card of the same suit, a card of the same number, or an eight), draws a card from the pile. (You may stipulate that players must continue to draw until a playable card is selected if the group is not larger than six people.) The play passes to the next student whose move is regulated by the last card played. The first student to play out all cards is the winner.

Variation One

For more speaking opportunities, add this element to the rules. When players discard to the point that they have only one remaining card, they must immediately announce, *I have only one card left!* If they forget, another player may say, *Draw two more!* Any player may make the penalty draw command when they see someone down to one card. Players are safe if they announce their one card status **before or even at the same time** as the *Draw two more!* command. The first student to play out all cards is the winner.

Variation Two

For more than 15 players, two people play as one. Each pair receives five to seven cards. One partner holds the cards or the two each take a few. The discarding begins as described in the original version. When the partners cannot play, either a penalty card is delivered or that element is eliminated entirely. Every pair calls out the suit and number loudly so the next partners will know how to continue the play.

Variation Three

Another option is to play Crazy Jacks, Crazy Aces, or any number of your choice. That card is played as the crazy card and has the power to change the suit to any other suit.

What Did Your Neighbor Play?

This versatile game can be used for any new or review material which can be depicted through drawings.

Purpose: Review or Introduction of Numbers, Nouns, Verbs, Phrases or Other Structures (Speaking, Optional Listening Comprehension Only)

Materials: Decks of student-made picture cards or numbered playing decks (2 decks for more than 10, 3 decks for more than 20)

Before the Game

Assemble 10 to 16 pictures or drawings depicting the target vocabulary. Fit the pictures on a single sheet of paper and photocopy one per student. Students can now make their own cards as described in *Make Your Own* on page 82.

Procedure

The object is to play out all cards. For more than 15 players, two students play as one in order to allow play to pass more quickly. Shuffle the number or picture cards all together and deal out five to seven to each player. More learning will take place if a player does not have more than one of the same card in a hand. Have a central pile of extra cards where students go to exchange any duplicates. Players should take care not to reveal the contents of their hands to the people on their right. With younger learners, however, (up to fourth grade), secrecy is not so important. They have difficulty manipulating the cards in their hands, so it is preferable to lay them out on the floor or on a desk so that they know at a glance what cards they have.

To begin, the first player discards any card face up on the floor or on a desktop and says, for example, *Seven* (if number cards are used) or *He's jumping* if picture cards are used. (In the comprehension stage, the teacher would make the description of the play.) The next person in line who has **that same card** plays it. The same player follows the first card with any other card, announcing the name (or repeating it after the teacher) as discarded. The third player is the next one in line who has a card matching the second card played by the previous player. Towards the end of the game, play may pass through the entire group and no one can match the last card. Play then returns to the person who last discarded.

To direct the play, the teacher repeatedly shows or acts out the meanings of the cards called and makes sure all know when their turns come. The first person to play out all cards is the winner.

Intermediate Games

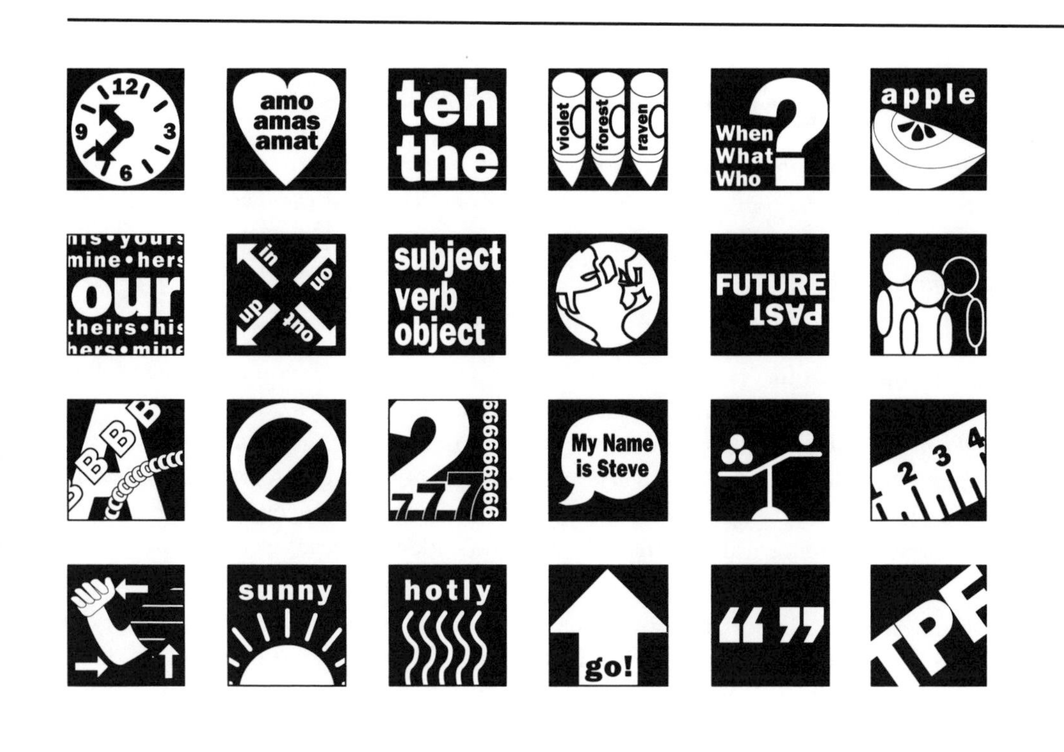

part 4 Intermediate Games

Getting Out of the Imperative

Teachers who begin with TPR sometimes find themselves using only commands and are unsure how to go about introducing other verb forms. Here are some entertaining ways to model and practice verbs in infinitive and conjugated form.

Conjugation Performances

This is a lively way to make verb drill fun and meaningful.

Purpose: Introduction and Review of Verb Forms, Sentences (Speaking)

Materials: Props that complement some verbs may be helpful (e.g., letter for "to mail," plane or bird for "to fly")

Before the Game

To introduce first person verb forms, ask students to give you a command, then describe aloud what you are doing as you do it. For example, a student says, *Jump over the wastebasket*. The teacher carries out the command, saying *I jump over the wastebasket*. In addition, describe your actions as you carry out daily classroom chores. *I answer the telephone, I return your homework, I open my book.* Utilize every opportunity to say what you are doing in all activities, allowing the students to hear first person frequently.

Large, colorful charts of verb forms posted around the room accelerate students' acquisition. It is important to frequently vary from the standard presentation of verbs in entire conjugations. Design charts to include a selected subject pronoun for several verbs, rather than a complete conjugation. If you have verb charts with complete conjugations, cover all forms except those you wish to emphasize.

Provide materials for students to create decorative verb posters. Consider making a *to have* wall and/or a *to be* wall, with conjugation posters and illustrated sentences covering all available space. Important and difficult verbs merit such publicity. Make sure you use separate walls if students tend to confuse the verbs.

Procedure

For "Conjugation Performances", divide the class into groups of five or six. List the verbs or announce the verb conjugation group you wish them to practice. Each group chooses a different verb and each member of the group composes a sentence which uses that verb and can be acted out. A few good examples from the teacher will start their creative juices flowing. Team members assist each other in the composition of the sentences. The teacher gives them a final check before students start to rehearse. They may utilize props or pictures if necessary to communicate the meanings.

The first performing group comes forward and each student says and acts his/her line in turn. They repeat the performance three times. For example, they have chosen the verb *to watch*. The first one says, *I watch television,* the next student says, *I watch movies.* The next students continue, *I watch girls, I watch the clock, I watch soap operas.* The first student starts the sequence again, *I watch television* and the others follow suit. Each time the sequence is repeated, it is in some way different from the preceding one, either in speed, pitch, volume or acting style. They might vary the three presentations from soft to loud, slow to fast, high to low in pitch, or from deadpan to overacting (or vice versa). One by one the groups perform their actions in front of the class, helping others within the group whenever needed.

Variation

Other verb forms should also be first used naturally in the class. Whenever you do things with students, describe your movements with *we.* Give narrative descriptions of individual and group actions to utilize *he, she* and *they.* When students are ready to practice the forms, "Conjugation Performances" works well for any of the subject pronouns.

Certain changes need to be made so that the pronouns are used according to their meanings. Partners within the group speak one sentence in unison when utilizing *we.* To practice *you, he, she,* or *they,* a student describes the actions of one or more other members of the group. Note that for natural use, the speaker talks **to fellow group members** when using *you* and **to the audience** when using *he, she* or *they.* For example, while the first student is running in place, the second student says, *S/he runs in place.* Then the second student drinks some milk and the first student says, *S/he drinks milk.* The third and fourth students follow with a description of each other's actions.

Conjugation Chants

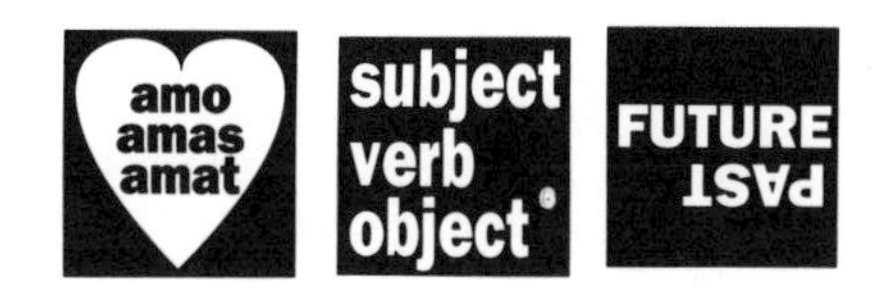

This game provides another route to repetition and reality without boredom.

Purpose: Review of Sentences, Verb Forms – Present, Past Tense (Speaking)

Materials: Props that complement some verbs may be helpful

Procedure

The class is divided into groups of five or six, and each group selects a different verb from a list provided by the teacher. The group members collectively compose a sentence using the verb which the group can act out (either individually or as a group). Except for real beginners, stipulate that the sentences must include more than just a subject and verb. Give examples of sentences with modifiers and phrases to make them longer. Model some accompanying actions to inspire them, especially if the group hasn't done the preceding activity, "Conjugation Performances".

Groups take a few minutes to plan and rehearse. Each sentence is chanted in rhythm four times. For example, a group of students sits on chairs or stools in front of the class, hold up their arms, pedal with their legs, and say in rhythm together, *We ride our bikes. We ride our bikes. We ride our bikes. We ride our bikes.* Then the teacher leads the class in the same chant but, of course, changed to *They ride their bikes. They ride their bikes. They ride their bikes. They ride their bikes.* The bike riders continue to perform, but do not speak while the class responds. When the *They* chant is completed, the bike riders stop the action.

Then starting with the end person, each student in turn rides one last time, saying, *I ride my bike.* After each student rides, the group chants back, *She rides her bike* or *He rides his bike.* In the beginning, the class will need some coaching on the correct responses before the chanting begins. The preparation will enable them to maintain a fairly steady rhythm and enjoy it more fully.

Variation One

For second person *you,* two groups (for example, the firemen and the mailmen) come forward and face each other. The mailmen act and chant, *We deliver the mail.* The firemen respond, *You deliver the mail.* The chant *We deliver the mail/You deliver the mail* is repeated four or five times. The firemen take the lead next, saying and acting out, *We put out fires.* The mailmen respond, *You put out fires.* The tandem chant is repeated the stipulated number of times. To add interest, vary the pace or volume as the chant progresses through the repetitions.

It is not necessary to use all subject pronouns for each verb each time you practice. You might do several verbs of one pattern or conjugation, using only one or two pronouns forms. Once students learn a conjugation, practice each form with verbs from other conjugations students have learned.

Variation Two

The chants can also be done in past tense or a combination of past and present. Be sure that students stop the action before a past tense chant begins.

apple

amo
amas
amat

Go Shopping

You may have played a game similar to this as a child: I'm going to Grandma's house and I'm taking...

Purpose: Introduction or Review of First Person Verb Forms, "To Buy," Nouns of Things You Buy (Speaking)

Materials: Props of items which can be purchased at a store, 2 large grocery bags

Procedure

In this memory game, students take turns shopping for items and playing the check-out clerk. Each shopper must name what the previous customers bought before they may add their purchase.

Display a group of items which could be purchased in a clothing store, grocery store, or any other store. There must be at least as many items as there are students. Next to the items, place two sacks large enough to hold all of the merchandise. For example, display and describe fruits and vegetables which are available at the market. To begin, the teacher approaches the food and says, *I go to the market and I buy a turnip, a banana, and a lemon* (or any other three items). The teacher holds up each item as named and puts them one at a time in one of the bags next to the fruits and vegetables. The teacher now becomes the checker in the store and sits in a chair facing the class, next to the food. A student shopper comes forward and says, *I go to the market and I buy* (the teacher coaches as often as needed for this beginning phrase) *a turnip, a banana, a lemon, ...* As a shopper says each item, the teacher/checker pulls it out of the bag, announcing and holding the item up for all to see and then transfers it to the other bag. Instruct the shopper to name the items slowly enough to allow the checker time to show and transfer the food. After successfully naming all items in the bag, the shopper selects and adds an item of his/her choice, for example, *and a beet.*

The teacher then gives up the checker's chair to the shopper who assumes that role. The second student comes forward. The shopper says the standard line, *I go to the market and I buy...,* and completes the sentence by naming (without looking into the bag) the preceding four foods in any order. The student checker removes and holds up each item as named, then transfers it to the other bag. After all items are transferred, the shopper adds another item of choice. The checker returns to the group, the shopper becomes the checker, and another shopper approaches.

It is not necessary to keep the same order in naming the items in the bag, only to name all of the previous purchases and then add one of the shopper's choice. If any shopper cannot name all of the already purchased items, students and the teacher give hints as to size, shape, color, use. Allow other students to give answers when shoppers are stumped. Students rotate through the roles of shopper and checker continuing play until everyone has had a turn to shop.

Variation One

To practice *We,* students work in partners. They say together, *We go to the market and we buy...* It is often better to do this form before the *I go* version because having a partner reduces stress.

Variation Two

To play competitively, divide class into teams of three or four people. Each group plays as one shopper, with team members helping each other. You could give teams the choice of saying in unison each time, *We go to the store...* or taking turns supplying the opener, *I go to the store...* Assistance from other group members is allowed either way. Points are awarded every time a team successfully completes the previous purchases and adds one of its own. No hints from the teacher or other teams this time.

Variation Three

Change the situation to enable practice of different vocabulary and structures. *I'm travelling to Spain (Germany, France, Japan) by boat (airplane, train, blimp). In my suitcase, I pack...* (one of the items displayed). Provide two suitcases and an assortment of clothing and other items that one might take along. Players choose different destinations and modes of transportation each time (according to their preferences), but must pack the same items as the previous travellers before adding an article of their choice. As items are named, another student makes the transfers from one suitcase to another.

Other possibilities include, *I open the treasure chest (purse, presents, surprise package) and I find...* (one of the items on display). *I go in the cave (house, barn, store) and I see ...* Invite students to contribute ideas for other situations.

Variation Four

If you don't wish to restrict the words practiced, and the students' vocabularies are large enough, have them complete the sentences with items starting with the letters of the alphabet in order. For example if English is the target language, the first student might *see (want, buy, find) an* ***a****pple,* the second, *an* ***a****pple and a* ***b****icycle,* the third, *an* ***a****pple, a* ***b****icycle, and a* ***c****oin,* etc.

Do As You Please

This versatile activity involves students in an interesting movement chain for verb practice. Changing the procedure slightly enables meaningful use of different subject pronouns and tenses.

Purpose: Introduction and Review of Verb Forms, Negative, Nouns (Speaking)

Materials: 6 or more picture flashcards depicting verbs or nouns which complement verbs

Procedure

Provide five or more students each with a picture illustrating a verb you wish to teach or review. The teacher also needs a picture. (Magazines are a good source of interesting pictures.) Limit the number of different verbs to the ability of your students. If you select only one verb, choose several pictures that could depict or complement the verb, but make them differ from each other. For example, if you are practicing the verb, *to go,* each student might have a picture of a different destination (which they have encountered previously). Students and teacher face the class standing in a straight line or, if everyone is participating, a circle. They hold the pictures in front of them so that others can see. The teacher reviews with the class the actions taking place in the pictures in first person verb form.

This version targets first person. For other subject pronouns, see the variations. To model the procedure, begin with your picture, holding it up and describing the action, for example, *I'm going (I go) to the theater.* Put the picture down, saying, *I'm not going to the theater,* and take the picture of the first student in line, showing and describing it, *I'm going to the beach.* Return the picture, saying, *I'm not going to the beach,* and take the second student's picture, *I'm going to the bakery.* Continue through the line of picture holders in this manner.

After modeling thoroughly, pick up your original picture and say, *I'm not going to the theater.* Put it back down and take any student's picture, claiming instead to do that action. The person left without a picture says, *I'm not going to* (whatever was taken away) and approaches anyone else in the line, saying, *"I'm going to* (the new picture). The students take the place of people from whom they take the flashcards each time and the chain is continued by the empty-handed student. The teacher assists with the responses and points out the choices when anyone needs help. The activity continues until everyone has participated several times. Closure may be brought by choosing the card that was played initially by the teacher; this leaves no one empty-handed.

To produce *we* naturally, students work with partners or groups of three and hold the same picture, saying, for example, *We're not going to the bakery. We're going home,* etc. Partners or groups speak together or rotate the task of speaking and selecting the next picture.

A more advanced level would have students holding pictures depicting several different verbs. The chain might sound like this: *I'm not brushing my teeth, I'm washing my face. I'm not washing my face, I'm taking a bath.*

Variation One

A similar format may be used for second person singular *(you)*. The participating students each receive a picture flashcard. The teacher approaches someone and exchanges cards, saying, *You're not* (the action on the student's card); *you're* (the action on the teacher's card). That student continues the chain by approaching and exchanging cards with another student.

Students work in partners and approach two people who hold one card to set up the use of plural *you.* Coach the students to speak directly to the pair from whom they take the cards, not to the audience. (If they speak to the audience, the natural subject would be third person.)

Variation Two

For *he* or *she,* use student actors, puppets, stuffed animals or pictures as the topics of conversation. Give a picture flashcard to everyone or a group standing in front. Students hold them so that others can see. A student who is selected to play the role of the King comes forward and faces the class holding a flashcard. The teacher begins by taking away the King's card, saying, *The King is not dancing.* The teacher takes another student's card, gives it to the King, saying, *He's playing tennis.* The empty-handed student says, *He's not playing tennis. He's reading a book,* as s/he takes back the tennis card and gives the reading picture to the King. The teacher gives several choices of actions on others' cards as students ponder the selection each time. Remind the students to speak to the audience, not to the puppets or people about which they are talking.

After everyone has participated, students exchange cards, choose a different King or Queen and the teacher begins another round.

There is nearly always someone in the class who will volunteer to play the role of the King, Queen or other personage. The monarch could wear a paper crown or the student might manipulate a puppet. Encourage them to act out whatever action is depicted in the picture.

To elicit *they,* use two or more puppets or people who face the class. Students carry out the card exchange as described, but refer to both people, *They're not ..., they're ...*

Variation Three

To provide practice for past tense, have a group of students do the activity in present tense, then reclaim their original pictures and repeat that same sequence of exchanges in the past tense, *I didn't go to the theater, I went to the beach.* The group helps one another to remember the order.

For a natural use of third person, students who were observing (or others in the participating group) relate the actions of those who made the picture exchanges, *S/he didn't go to the theater, s/he went to the beach. We* and *they* are accomplished by using more than one student as described in the original version.

For future tense, set up imaginary (realistic is possible, but more difficult) future situations that accommodate the pictures you have in play. Students begin their description of the cards with such phrases as, *In ten years..., In my next life..., Someday...*

The Class Against the Duck

This guessing game can be tailored to fit beginning or more accomplished speakers. The first version is less advanced and is more fun if you use a puppet with a mouth that can open and grab.

Purpose: Third Person Verb Forms, Nouns, Questions and Answers, Adjectives, Adverbs, Phrases or Other Structures (Speaking)

Materials: Puppet with mouth that opens, large picture flashcards

Procedure

A student volunteers to be the Duck or any other animal puppet with a mouth that can open and grab. Since the animal does not have a speaking role and yet is in the limelight, it is a good position for less advanced students. The teacher and the Duck sit facing the class with a stack of large picture flashcards placed near them. The class need not have seen the pictures before, but be prepared to act out the meaning of any new vocabulary through gestures and actions. The animal competes with classmates who try to guess what is on the cards.

The teacher turns up a card, and showing it only to the Duck, makes two statements about the picture. One accurately fits the picture, the other does not. Descriptive sentences for a picture of a dog sitting might be, for example, *The dog walks* and *The dog sits.* (You could also make a question, *Is the dog walking or sitting?*) The first student in the class (student pair if you have a large class) guesses one of the choices given and the teacher then shows the card, saying whatever it depicts.

If the guess is correct, the card is awarded to the class. If the choice is incorrect, the Duck takes it in its beak. The teacher draws a second card and gives a choice of descriptive words or sentences to the next student guesser. The game continues until all have had a chance to guess. Everyone counts the number of cards at the end to determine the winner.

The questions or statements used can vary according to the teacher's objective. *Is the girl happy or sad?* (adjectives). *A peach or a pumpkin?* (nouns). *The bird is in the nest or next to the nest?* (prepositions). *Is the boy walking swiftly or slowly?* (adverbs). *The man ate or the man is eating ?* (tense). *Is the Jolly Green Giant bigger than the bean stalk or smaller than the bean stalk?* (comparative).

Variation

For more advanced speakers, play a team game. Divide the students into two groups, such as the Kangaroos vs. the Camels. Assign partners within the teams. Each pair receives a picture card which they must not show to anyone on the other team. The two teams may wish to form a huddle to ensure secrecy. Partners compose two statements—one true and one false. One sentence must accurately describe the picture; the false one may be similar or it may be very different. Encourage students to seek help from other group members. To make sure they remember the two sentences, they may write them on paper. The teacher circulates to assist and check for errors. Those undetected may be corrected as they come up in the game. Convert faulty sentences to correct form without focusing on the errors or forcing the students to repeat the corrected version.

The guessing works best if the teams face each other so that body language clues can be spotted. A Kangaroo pair states their two descriptive sentences loudly to a Camel pair. Encourage naturally loud volume by matching Kangaroo speakers with Camels who are sitting far from them rather than near to them. The Camels repeat the one which they think accurately describes the picture the Kangaroos are holding. If correct, the picture is taken from the Kangaroos and begins the pile of points for the Camels. If incorrect, the Kangaroos are awarded the picture and it starts their winning pile. The next two Kangaroos give their choices to the next two Camels. When the Kangaroos are out of pictures, the roles switch and the Camels give choices to the Kangaroos. Teams count the number of pictures accumulated at the end to determine the winner.

After each guess, take time to pass the picture in front of the entire group, repeating the students' sentence that described the picture. The pictures are of interest to the entire group, because everyone wants to see for themselves if it was *an owl in a tree* or *an owl in a cage.*

To Say or Not To Say

This quick cure for mindless repetition requires that you think about what you say before you say it.

Purpose: Introduction or Review of Verb Forms, Review of Nouns (Speaking)

Materials: 12 to 20 large objects, numbers or pictures

Procedure

The activity works best if played with objects or a mixture of objects and numbers. Pictures can be used if they are large and quickly identifiable. The teacher holds up and describes various objects. The students' task is to repeat all correct descriptions and say nothing if any part of the teacher's description is incorrect. For example, the teacher holds up a green hat and says loudly, *(I have) A green hat!* The class chimes back, *(You have) A green hat!* The teacher does several more correctly (to establish the pattern of repetition) but then holds up a red sock and says, *(I have) A red shirt!* No one should say anything. Many goofs will be made, and good-natured laughter is appropriate.

Each item is *won* by the class if information repeated is true. If there are any goofs (if **anyone** repeats false information), the teacher wins the object or picture. The teacher also wins the item if the class hesitates in repetition of a correct description or if the class response is very weak. At the end, the two piles—teacher's and students'—are counted to determine a winner.

The verb should be kept constant for at least 10 or more teacher/student exchanges. At this point the teacher could choose a different verb. Hold up pictures or props of people in different professions, for example, and say, *I am a doctor*. The class replies, *You are a doctor*, etc. Other situations might be *I eat...* (different foods); *I go to bed* or *get up at...* (different times); *I play the...* (different musical instruments); *I like ...* (different sports or leisures).

Variation One

Change the procedure slightly to utilize other verb forms. For a second person plural response from the class, the teacher takes a partner and the two of them say, *We like...* To practice third person, one or two students hold up the pictures. The teacher points to the student(s) and picture(s), saying *s/he likes...* or *they like...* The class chimes back in the same person.

Variation Two

For large classes, or to vary the game, divide students into teams of three to six people. The smaller groups keep the less vocal people from being drowned out by the crowd. Each team takes turns collectively responding to five or six items at a time. The team wins the objects named correctly. Incorrect repetitions are returned to the pile for future play. The team with the most accumulated items at the end of the game is the winner.

Chain Relay

A variety of expressions or structures may be practiced in this high-interest, competitive activity.

Purpose: Verb Forms, Questions and Answers, Nouns, Expressions, or Other Structures (Speaking; Optional Writing)

Materials: Chalkboard, an object or small expendable picture for each student

Procedure

This game is easily made more or less advanced by the length and complexity of the phrases or structures the teacher selects. Teams compete to be the first to pass phrases or oral exchanges in a chain from one end of a line of players to the other. Play the original version or Variation One if you have accomplished speakers. Use the modifications explained in Variation Two if some students need assistance.

Divide the students into teams of seven to ten members. Groups line up separately or sit in different rows. Position the groups so that the end or last players are all sitting at equal distances from a designated place in the front of the room. When writing is included in the activity, the end players should be at equal distances from the blackboard.

The teacher selects vocabulary to be targeted, for example, the verb *to have* and *body ailments*. In a vertical column on the board, sketch seven to ten parts of the body—the same number as there are players on a team. If the teams have seven people each, draw seven body parts, perhaps a head, back, leg, teeth, foot, knee and stomach. Practice the parts on the board in an appropriate dialogue with the entire class, for example, *How are you feeling? I have a... ache.*

Starting with the first people in line, assign different body ailments corresponding to the order the body parts are drawn on the board. Players in first position all have headaches, second position have back aches, third have leg aches, etc.

To begin play, a signal is given and the first people in each line say to the second, *I have a headache. How are you feeling?* The second people respond, *I have a back ache.* The second person then turns to the third person and says, *How are you feeling?* The third person answers, *I have a leg ache,* and asks the fourth, *How are you feeling?* The question/answer process continues to the final person who answers, then immediately runs to the board and writes his/her ailment, *I have a...* If writing is not a goal, have the end student deliver the team mascot to a front table or other designated place.

As soon as the words are written on the board or the mascot is delivered, the players return to their seats as quickly as possible. The first one(s) to sit down yell(s), *Stop!* to the other teams. The team to complete the process ahead of the others receives one point. In case of a tie, both teams receive a point. An additional point is awarded if the sentence is written with no errors. Any team who completes the writing before *Stop!* is eligible for a correct sentence point.

Encourage students to help each other if teammates forget their lines; the teacher may also assist. All players must complete the dialogue. The players last in line may have the sentence written on paper to study. They may look at the sentence they are to write until the moment they leave their places and go to the board.

The students now rotate positions within the team; the last player moves to the first chair and all others move over or down one place. Each team member now has a new ailment, according to the order of the drawings on the board. The teacher repeats the ailments and students practice their new lines before the next round. Give the last people instructions to write either the same sentence or assign a different one.

Variation One

This activity is extremely versatile and may be changed slightly to practice other structures. Pass out an assortment of small objects representing target vocabulary. The props serve the same function as the drawings on the board did in the above activity. Each member of the chain says, *I have the (toothbrush), What do you have?*

In the absence of objects—or to use expressions of weather, time, destinations, etc.– use small expendable pictures from blackline masters in *Basic Vocabulary Builder* and *Practical Vocabulary Builder, 1000 Pictures for Teachers to Copy*. (See *Paper Props, Flashcards* in the *Sources* section.) You might give them pictures of people in different professions and have them say, *I am a fireman, Are you a fireman?* A pilot is next in line and responds, *No, I'm not a fireman, I'm a pilot.* The pilot then turns to the next student and says, *I'm a pilot. Are you a pilot?* Students rotate after each round but the props or pictures stay with the chairs.

Variation Two

Lack of skill may present problems for beginning speakers. In order to assist those who have difficulty, the teacher moves down the line of speakers as the dialogue is passed, prompting students as needed. Since the teacher can monitor only one team at a time, the other teams (non-speakers) are assigned an activity which does not require the teacher's attention, such as drawing at the board.

The task for the non-speakers can be related in content to the speakers' assigned dialogue, or it can be totally different. The non-speakers could draw the parts of a body while the speakers pass on what time they have on their clocks.

For a review of body parts, for example, the teacher assigns each non-speaker a part of the body. Player one might have the head, player two the eyes, player three the nose, etc. The parts can be listed in a column on the board, or give each student a picture to ensure that all remember their assignment. If there is more than one team of non-speakers, the assignment should be the same for each if the vocabulary is fairly new. For review, use different vocabulary for each team.

The teacher helps the speakers rehearse their lines. Positioned ready to monitor the first speaker, the teacher gives the signal for everyone to begin. As the speakers begin their dialogue, the first members of the non-speaking team run to the board, draw the head, then run back and tag the next team members. The second in line run to the board, draw the eyes and run back to tag the third people. The runners may not move from their seats until tagged. The teacher can rely on the observations of the speaking team to make sure that the drawing team abides by the rules.

The non-speakers continue to draw until the speaking team (under the guidance of the teacher) has completed their dialogue chain. The last speaker runs to the board to write the assigned word(s). (Eliminate this if the group is not yet writing.) The last speaker then yells, *Stop!* to the non-speakers.

Each body part drawn up to that point earns one point for the drawing teams. Team by team, the drawing groups call out in unison (or individually) the names of each body part as the teacher points them out on their drawings. With each part named, include a running total of the points so the end score will be known when the last part is identified. The teacher and the class now inspect any words written on the board by the speakers. If there are any errors, each non-speaking team receives an additional point. The scores are recorded and the teams rotate positions within the team, the last person becoming the first and everyone else moving back (over) one chair. The speaking role now goes to an opposing team. All others are drawers. Points are scored only by the non-speaking (drawing) teams.

Variation Three

Activities other than drawing are possible for non-speaking teams. Team members might put on assigned articles of clothing while the teacher is monitoring the speaking team. The teacher assigns each non-speaking team member an article from a line of clothing in front of the room. The first item (for player one) might be a shoe (two or more shoes if there is more than one non-speaking team). The second item(s) in line would be for player two. While the teacher is monitoring the dialogue of the speaking team, other teams run to put on the preassigned items, then run back (wearing the clothing) and tag the next players who run to put on their items. Points are awarded to the teams dressing: one point for each item of clothing players have put on and can name. As they remove the clothing one by one, each student names the item or says, *I take off...* Clothing items are returned to the lineup in front of the room for the next round and players rotate positions.

Variation Four

Materials: A number flashcard for each non-speaking team member

Another possible activity for non-speaking teams is a number review. Pass out one number flashcard to each student. On each flashcard a different number is written out, such as, *thirty-two, sixty-one,* etc. As the teacher monitors the speaking team, the opposing team members run to the board one at a time and write out their numbers in digit form, *32*, *62*, etc. When the speakers are finished, non-speakers who wrote the numbers call them out as the teacher points to each number on the board. One point is scored for each number correctly written and identified. Students rotate positions so that they will have different numbers on the next round.

Charades

Dramatization is an important path to long-term memory. Charades provide entertaining practice for nouns, verbs, adjectives, adverbs and many expressions. Start with a group charade, so that shy students will be willing to take part.

Category Charades

A good warm-up for timid actors—no one is on stage alone in this group charade.

Purpose: Review of Nouns, Verbs, Adjectives, Adverbs, Phrases or Other Structures (Speaking)

Materials: None

Procedure

Charades come naturally to teachers who are accustomed to making their output comprehensible. Take the time to plan and rehearse your presentation to the students; it is the key to stimulating creative juices and making the activity flow.

For charade topics, the teacher selects four or five review categories of nouns, verbs, adjectives, adverbs or expressions. Adverbs might be a category in itself, whereas you would name subcategories of nouns (clothing, furniture, professions). Whatever the categories, spend some time brainstorming words in each category with the class. They may be pleasantly surprised by the number of words their collective memory can produce. Model how to charade, acting out at least two words (those you have preplanned) from each category. No props, sounds or words may be used. Continue acting until students guess correctly.

Discuss how dramatization might be done as a group rather than individually. Suppose a group chooses to act out *table*. One person could assume a body posture in an upside-down, squared U shape, and others could be chairs or do actions suitable to a table (set it, polish it, eat from it). Another approach would have some people forming the legs and another be the top.

Divide the class into teams of three to five people. They choose team names and form a huddle to select their category and word in secrecy. The teams discuss and rehearse strategies for conveying the meaning without using words or props.

The first team to present stands before the class and the remaining teams take turns guessing the category. Each successive team gets one guess until the category is correctly named. The team which successfully names the category is awarded a point and a bonus guess. Now the acting begins.

Members within a team take turns guessing the item being acted out; the guesser may accept suggestions from other team members. Pass the team mascot within the team so that everyone knows whose turn it is to guess. Establish a time limit (less than a minute) for a team to produce a guess. When the time is up or an incorrect guess is made, the play passes to the team next in line.

Guessing continues until a group names the word being performed or each team has had one to three guesses (depending on the number of words they know in that category and the number of teams). A successful guess earns a point. To encourage good acting, award one point to each charade team that successfully conveys the meaning. The goal is to communicate, not to fool the audience. No points are awarded if the class does not guess in the stipulated number of guesses. Play continues until all teams have acted at least once. Decide what to do if actors accidentally speak or break the rules. They could choose another word or pass the play to the next team.

Variation

Materials: Pictures of categories of nouns, adjectives, verbs, adverbs, phrases or other structures

For more acting challenge, require students to act out the word or picture they draw from a pile, rather than make their own selection.

Fish Charades

This game combines considerable challenge with kid-like fun.

Purpose: Review of Verbs, Nouns, Sentences, Phrases and Other Structures (Speaking, Reading, Optional Writing)

Materials: Colored construction paper, paper clips, scissors, fishing pole with magnet on end of line

Students take turns catching paper fish on which are written sentences, then acting out the meanings of the sentences. The first version is for students who are writing. Consult the Variation if your learners are less advanced. Do not be put off by older students who associate paper-fishing with young children. Assure them that challenging material presented in a fun fashion facilitates memory.

Before the Game

As a homework assignment or class activity, students write ten simple sentences whose meaning can be communicated through props and actions. Stipulate the verbs and vocabulary which you want them to utilize in the sentences and demonstrate how to mime several different combinations. The sentences could begin with nouns or pronouns. Any of the subject pronouns can be acted out by pointing to oneself, a boy or a girl, or a group of males and/or females. Have students brainstorm ways to act out the distinction between familiar and formal if this is an element in your target language. Collect the papers and correct the sentences.

When the corrected sentences are returned, divide the class into teams of three to six people. Provide colored construction paper, paper clips and scissors. Everyone draws and cuts out five fish, about four inches in length. If possible, provide teams with different colored paper in order to easily identify their fish. If not, have them select and draw a symbol representing their team on the back of each fish. One side is left blank. Give specific directions for drawing and cutting, making the process and materials used a part of the learning. Each student chooses five of the corrected sentences to write on the blank side of his/her paper fish–only one sentence per fish. A paper clip is attached to the head of each fish.

Procedure

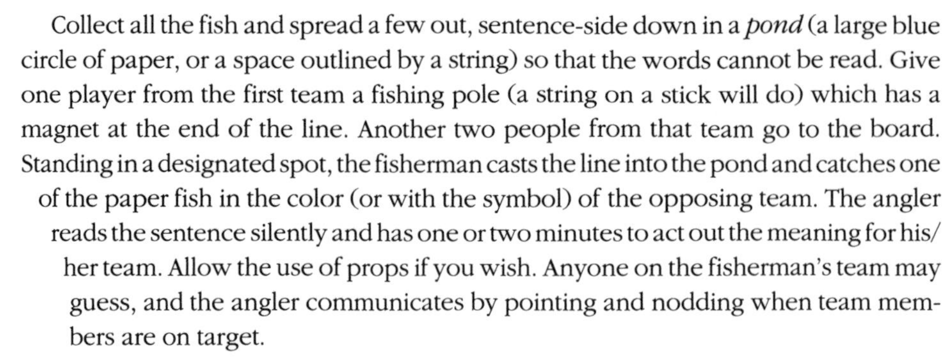

Collect all the fish and spread a few out, sentence-side down in a *pond* (a large blue circle of paper, or a space outlined by a string) so that the words cannot be read. Give one player from the first team a fishing pole (a string on a stick will do) which has a magnet at the end of the line. Another two people from that team go to the board. Standing in a designated spot, the fisherman casts the line into the pond and catches one of the paper fish in the color (or with the symbol) of the opposing team. The angler reads the sentence silently and has one or two minutes to act out the meaning for his/her team. Allow the use of props if you wish. Anyone on the fisherman's team may guess, and the angler communicates by pointing and nodding when team members are on target.

The two players at the board write the correctly named elements on the board as they are guessed. Help is allowed from other team members. The team can score up to five points for oral production of a sentence (don't penalize for minor mispronunciations) and another five points for the written version. Points are fewer than five according to the number of parts not guessed orally or words incorrectly spelled on the written version. Points might be deducted for every two mistakes if your sentences are lengthy.

Play passes to the next team and replacement fish are added to the pond as needed. The role of the fisherman rotates among team members.

Variation

For less advanced and younger students, the teacher may need to write the sentences on the fish, perhaps all in command form. The students still draw and cut out the fish. For beginners, it is often better to eliminate the competition and make it a class effort to come up with the sentences or commands written on the fish. The angler may also need an assistant to help act out the sentence.

amo amas amat

Combination Charades

Words need to be mixed and recombined in many ways for increased comprehension. This activity combines fantasy and reality for a whole brain experience.

Purpose: Review of Second and Third Person Verb Forms, Nouns (Reading, Speaking, Optional Writing)

Materials: Chalkboard

List in a column on the board a dozen or more verbs (use second person singular) which can be acted out. Next to the verbs, write a column of nouns which could be used, with some imagination, in various combination with the verbs.

The list might look like this:

you are	*opening*	*the door*
	closing	*the window*
	hitting	*the dragon*
	sitting on	*the chair*
	walking to	*the table*
	hiding	*the pen*
	walking	*the dog*
	cutting	*the cake*

The teacher reviews the meanings of the words by acting each one out (in random order). The class guesses as the teacher dramatizes.

Procedure

To model a combined charade, select an item from both columns to act out. No words or props may be used. Students try to figure out which combination the teacher has chosen and announce guesses, such as, *You're running to the window, You're throwing the chair,* etc. The more dramatic the teacher is, the better. Sometimes the meaning is better communicated by acting out the noun before the verb. The teacher's gestures indicate whether the guesses are all or partially incorrect. The class continues to guess and the teacher continues to act until the correct combination is voiced. Correct guessers or volunteers are chosen to act out the next sentence of their own combination.

Encourage them to have fun with silly combinations, such as the following:

you are	*opening*	*the flower*
	closing	*the hat*
	hitting	*the cake*
	sitting on	*the dog*
	walking	*the dragon*
	eating	*the window*
	throwing	*the table*

Variation One

For second person plural, change verb forms on the board. Student actors present the charade in pairs or trios. The audience directs guesses to both actors.

Variation Two

For third person (s/he, they), the students write their charade sentences in advance and give them to the teacher or leader before they perform. The class directs guesses to the teacher or a student leader, calling for *s/he* statements about a single performer and *they* statements for a pair or group of the charaders. The charade performers do not respond to the guesses since they are being talked **about,** not addressed.

Bottle Charades

This takeoff on spin the bottle is a winner with all old enough to read and write.

Purpose: Second Person and Third Person Verb Forms, Commands, Nouns, Student-Selected Phrases or Other Structures (Speaking, Reading, Writing)

Materials: Bottle, floor space

Procedure

Provide students with several examples of charade commands. The commands must be actions that can be communicated without props. *Dig a hole. Open a bottle of Coke and drink it. Climb a ladder,* etc. After several inspiring examples from the teacher, students compose five to ten of their own charade commands and write them on paper (to hand in for correction, if you wish). Stipulate the verbs and other vocabulary you want them to incorporate in the commands. After correction by peers or the teacher, each student selects two favorites and writes one each on a half sheet of paper, signing his/her name to each. Collect and shuffle the papers.

Students sit in a circle with a bottle and the command papers and in the middle. For large groups, see Variation Two. Someone spins the bottle to select the first charader. The player indicated draws from the paper pile, announces the author, and reads the command silently. (Players who draw their own papers draw again.) The player performs the command using no words, sounds or props. Students direct their guesses to the charader, *You're wrapping a package!* or *You're eating an apple!* The author of the command may not guess but may help with the acting if the group has trouble guessing.

The person who performed the charade gets the privilege of making the next spin to see who the next actor will be. If the bottle points to a person who has already performed, play passes to the closest person (on the left or right) who has not yet participated.

Variation One

To practice third person, *He's wrapping a package!* or *She's eating an apple!,* the actor draws a command and gives it to the author. The class directs guesses to the author, not the actor. The actor must refrain from indicating correctness of the group's responses. The teacher lends assistance in supplying the correct verb forms or pronunciation when necessary.

Variation Two

If your group is too large to sit in a circle on available floor space, put half of them in the circle and assign partners who sit or stand directly behind. The bottle points to the ones in the circle. They draw the commands and enlist their partners' assistance in performing them. Using two performers provides practice for *you* plural, if guesses are addressed to the actors, and *they,* if directed to the author. Upon completion, the one who drew the command spins, then the two switch places and the partner from behind sits in the circle. Play passes to the left or right after a pair has performed twice.

Spelling Games

Spelling is difficult for most students, necessitating a variety of interesting ways to practice. Provide extra incentive by announcing in advance when a game will be played and stipulating the vocabulary involved.

Back Writing

This activity for beginning spelling works especially well with languages using pictographic characters in their alphabet. Begin with a demonstration for the entire class, then facilitate work in pairs.

Purpose: Spelling (Writing, Reading)

Materials: Chalkboard or handouts of words

Procedure

Select five or more words on the board. To increase the difficulty of the task, increase the number of words and have several which begin with the same letter. It is imperative that all students see the words clearly. To accomplish this you may need to provide each student with a copy of the words.

Two volunteers come forward. One stands behind the other and both face the words on the board (or hold the lists in front of them) with their backs to the class. One is to be the Writer or the Chalk, and the other is the Chalkboard. (You may wish to say that one is the Pen or Pencil, and the other is the Paper.) The Chalk silently chooses a word from the list to print on the back of the Chalkboard partner. The Chalk may use a finger or any blunt instrument, such as the eraser end of a pencil or a capped pen. Writing should be done slowly and in as large a print as the back will allow. In order for the class to observe the writing, the Chalk should stand to the side (not in front) of the Chalkboard and write at arm's length.

Write up or down, left to right or right to left according to the way the language is normally written. The letters in long words may have to be split into more than one line or column. The Chalkboard may request that the word be written again or more slowly if necessary. If the Chalkboard is unable to guess the word being written, the audience helps out. A correct guess may entitle the Chalkboard to become the Chalk if s/he chooses, and another Chalkboard is selected. If the class is large, two writers and two backs may be necessary, positioned so that the process can be seen by everyone and can involve all students.

After a few examples in front of the class, divide the class into partners. Tell them to decide which one of the partners is the Chalkboard and which one is the Chalk and to position themselves for writing. The pairs may want to sit on their desks or stand in order to facilitate writing. Both are positioned so that they can see the master list. Students could make their own copies for practice and easier viewing. The Chalk writes a word from the list on the back of the Chalkboard. Chalkboards who have difficulty deciphering the writing direct the Chalk to repeat words more slowly and in bigger letters. The Chalk may need to give clues as to the location of the word, for example, *in the first half of the list* or *in the last five sentences.* Teach the Chalk to say, *Guess again!,* instead of, *No!* Teach the Chalkboards to say, *Repeat more slowly, please,* and *Give me a hint.* After the Chalk have written three or four words, they switch roles and the same procedure is followed.

Variation One

To double the writing practice, direct the Chalkboards to write the words on paper, as they feel them on their backs. This time the Chalkboards do not look at the master list. The Chalkboards then say and show the words to the Chalk, and they both verify the spelling from the master list.

Variation Two

For variety try writing on other parts of the body (arm, palm or back of the hand) and compare the different results. Nerve endings are closer together in some places, like the palm of the hand; such body parts are therefore more sensitive. Does this make it easier to decipher the letters?

Spelling Toss

Spelling seems to come more easily when combined with throwing.

Purpose: Review of Nouns, Spelling of Nouns (Writing, Speaking)

Materials: Box or wastebasket, props which can be thrown without damage, paper sack, floor space

Procedure

In this active and exciting team game, students work in pairs to spell vocabulary words and toss the corresponding objects in a container.

Select objects which can be tossed about without breaking, such as stuffed or rubber animals or plastic fruits and vegetables. You need at least half as many objects as there are students.

Divide the class into two groups which each select a team name from props you provide. Each team forms partners within the group. Review the objects with the class as you place the items in a bag. Two pairs begin, one from each team. Each team has one person at the board and another in throwing position, eight to twelve feet back from the board. Using tape or chalk, make a line on the floor in front of the throwers. Place a large box to receive the tossed objects between the two board players. (See diagram.) The teacher stands between the throwing players with the bag of objects.

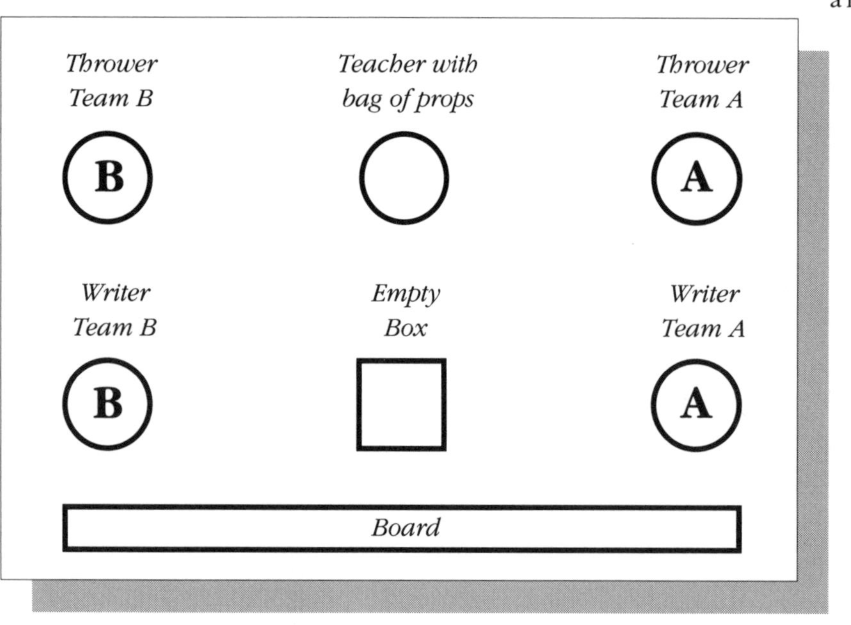

On a signal, the teacher simultaneously pulls out two items from the bag and gives one to each thrower. As soon as they are visible, the throwers shout the name of the object (with the help of the other team members when needed) to the partners at the board who write the word as quickly as possible. The writers may not look at the items but throwers may repeat the names as many times as they wish. The teacher joins in the repetitions of the words when students need help in exact pronunciations. You might permit the throwing partners (remaining in position) to also call out the spelling if the writers have difficulty. Other team members may nod agreement or disapproval of how the word is spelled, but they may not give out letters. It becomes too chaotic if everyone helps.

As soon as the writing is finished, the writers put down the chalk and turn around. The throwers may then attempt to toss the props into the box. If the throwers miss the box, **the writers** retrieve the objects and give or toss it back to the throwers who try again. The throwers many not advance beyond the line. The partners continue to retrieve and toss until the objects go into the box.

The first team to successfully pitch the item into the box wins a point. If their word is spelled correctly, it is an additional point. A team also gets a point if they spell the word correctly even though they are not the first to hit the box. When the sack is empty, objects may be exchanged or recycled for a second round. The team with the most points is declared the winner.

Alphabet Challenge

This game offers fun and challenge for students learning the alphabet.

Purpose: Spelling, Alphabet (Comprehension, Writing)

Materials: Chalkboard

Procedure

For this activity, students should have had previous exposure to the alphabet but need not be proficient. Select words which students know orally, but they need not be words which they have seen written. Reading and writing words not previously seen is a satisfying accomplishment.

Two volunteers go to the board. Without pronouncing the word, the teacher orally spells one or two short words in the target language. The students at the board write the word(s) as quickly as they can. To help them, the rest of the class is invited to call out the word(s) as soon as they recognize it by the teacher's spelling, but they may not help the writer with the individual letters. The teacher repeats the spelling until one of the students writes it correctly. The teacher indicates errors by emphasizing incorrect letters when respelling the word. Invite class members to contribute to the error detection by calling out letters when they think someone has written them incorrectly.

Variation

Play the game competitively by forming two teams equal in number. Players race to write the words correctly. Place two chairs five to ten feet from the board. Representatives from opposing teams sit in the chairs and listen as the teacher spells a word with eight or fewer letters (without announcing what the word is). As soon as the entire word is spelled, the teacher signals for them to go to the board and write. Team members help, but only by calling out the word if they know it and indicating whether they think the word is written correctly or not.

Students return to their chairs as soon as they are satisfied with what they have written. The first player to write the word correctly and sit down is replaced by another team member. The player who came in second has the opportunity to try the next word. If neither player is correct, they both remain to receive another word. After three unsuccessful tries, players automatically rotate. Give easier words on second and third attempts. The winning team is the one which rotates the entire team through its speller's chair.

Disappearing Letters

A competitive group effort helps students to focus on spelling.

Purpose: Spelling, Alphabet (Reading, Writing)

Materials: Chalkboard, two colors of chalk, number cards

Procedure

This activity can be adapted for beginning or advanced spellers, depending on the number of words or phrases used and the number of letters which disappear. See the Variation if you wish to include practice using the alphabet.

Write five to ten words or phrases on the board and assign each a number. Use numbers students need to review. Make a deck of numbers which corresponds to the numbers assigned to the words on the board.

In random order, call out the numbers and have student volunteers read the words aloud. The teacher or students demonstrate the meanings through actions and props.

Divide the class into teams of three to five people. Announce that in one minute (or more), you will erase some of the letters in each word or phrase. The students' task will be to replace them. Without writing, the students memorize the spelling of as many as they can. At the end of the stipulated time for study, the teacher erases one to five letters per word, perhaps leaving a minimum of three letters in long words and one letter in short words. Draw a short line on the board in place of every letter you remove. Vary the number of erasures to match the skill of the group. Erase fewer letters if the words are new; more if they are review.

The first player draws a number from the deck and has 10 or 15 seconds to confer with team members. At the end of the time, the player announces the number and the word. When either the number or the word is incorrect, the number is returned to the deck and the play passes to the next team. If the combination is correct, ie. number and word, the player goes to the board to fill in the missing letters, using a different color. A player who advances to the board may not receive additional help from team members.

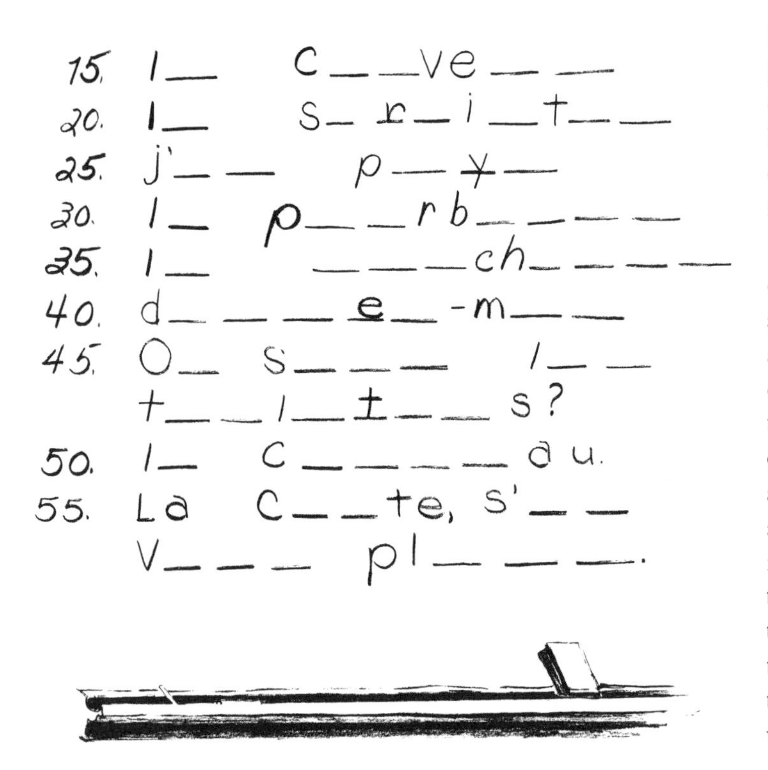

Allow imperfections in pronunciation when students announce their words, but be sure to continually announce the word during the writing so that students have maximum opportunity to hear it correctly. If the missing letters are filled in correctly, the team is awarded a point. If the word is incorrect, or any part of the phrase is incorrect, all of the student's letters are erased and the word or phrase is available for the next team. The teacher may announce how many errors were made. Play passes to the next team whether or not the point is scored. The task of spelling rotates among team members. Each team passes a mascot (representing the name of the team) among the team members to keep track of whose turn is next.

When all words and phrases have been attempted, fill in the letters of those no one could spell (if any) and use them in the next round. The team who accumulates the most points is the winner. If additional rounds are played, rotate the order in which teams play since the teams at the beginning have the advantage of having to remember a shorter period of time.

Variation

To focus on the alphabet **as well as** spelling, play as described except require students to call out the missing letters in the target language. The teacher writes whatever a student says (if it is comprehensible), right or wrong. All team members may help the designated speller come up with the correct letters. The teacher writes only what the speller says.

The missing letters must be supplied in the same order as they appear in the words and the speller may guess only once for each blank. If a mistake is made in supplying a letter, the play stops at that letter and passes to an opposing team. Erase all letters written before the mistake was made. A team which correctly completes a word is awarded one point.

In this version, you may either allow teams to select their own words or assign them numbers and provide corresponding numbered cards for students to draw.

Shoot and Score

The problem with traditional spelldowns is that they eliminate the poor spellers, the ones who need most to be involved. This version eliminates no one, provides support for the weak spellers and enables those who are more physically inclined to also shine.

Purpose: Review of Alphabet, Spelling (Speaking)

Materials: Ball and wastebasket

Procedure

This game requires students to be fairly accomplished in using the letters, especially if you ask them to spell phrases rather than single words. Foreign language teachers have the option of allowing students to spell in their first language until they become more accomplished.

Divide the class into two teams, for example, the Bears and the Leopards. All the Bears and Leopards choose a partner on the same team. Place a wastebasket in the front of the room. Mark a spot on the floor eight to fifteen feet away, from which players throw a ball. Make sure the basket is positioned far enough from the mark to present some challenge but not so far that most will miss it.

The teacher pronounces a word or phrase from a spelling list to the first Leopard partners. They consult with each other for a limited time; use of paper and pencil is allowed. One of the partners goes to the board without the paper. The partner at the board writes the word on the board as it is spelled aloud by the other partner. If correct, one of the partners attempts to shoot a ball into a wastebasket. If incorrect, no shots are taken, and play passes to the opposing team. A successful shot gives the Leopards **two** points. If the first partner misses the basket, the second partner shoots for **one** point. After two misses, play passes to the opposing team.

Incorrectly spelled words are corrected by a volunteer or the teacher and become part of a running list of *words to be repeated* on the board. Once you have five corrected words on the board, erase them and re-enter them on the list of words to be given. Play always passes to the opposing team after partners attempt to spell a word, whether or not they are successful.

Students waiting for a turn may study from individual spelling lists or vocabulary sections of their texts, noting those words on the board which will be used again. Partners may not use their lists or receive help (except from a partner) during their turn. The teacher calls the words in a different order from the one on the study list.

Variation

Calling of the words may be done by the teams instead of the teacher. The Bears would give the Leopards a word, then vice versa. Any caller may receive help in pronunciation from other team members or the teacher.

Words in Containers

A cooperative approach enables students who normally do not like memory games to enjoy this one.

Purpose: Nouns, Spelling, Verb Forms – Past, Present, Future (Speaking, Reading, Writing)

Materials: One object for each student or every two students, 2 different containers (each large enough to accommodate half of the objects), handout for each student with all objects listed

Before the Game

A discussion of thinking strategies for memorization is appropriate preparation for this game. Instruction in visualization and association techniques can improve memory and will also lead to improved test scores. A good reference for both teachers and students (junior high and older) is *Use Your Perfect Memory* by Tony Buzan. Although upper elementary students might not read the book, they could benefit from the teacher's instruction in these strategies.

Procedure

Select a group of nouns or other vocabulary which can be represented by an object. Pictures will work but the three-dimensional objects are more fun and easier to remember. The students' task is to put objects in containers and then try to list the contents in each container from memory.

Students sit in a circle or two equal lines facing each other. Scatter a group of objects, one per student, in the middle of the group. If you assign partners, you need only half as many objects as you have students. Review the list of words with the class, perhaps matching up the displayed objects with flashcards of the words. Next to the objects place two different containers, such as a pillow case and a covered basket.

Coach the entire group on one or more standard phrase(s) to be utilized in playing the game, such as, *I place (will place) the … in the …, I take (will take) the …,* or *I choose (will choose) the …* When the class is comfortable with the chosen line, ask for an assistant to help you in teaching the next part of the game dialogue. The assistant places items one at a time in one container or the other. The class describes each action, *S/he places (placed) the … in the …, s/he takes (took) the …,* or *s/he chooses (chose) the …* When the class is accomplished enough to respond quickly in chorus the game begins.

Give the pillow case to one team and the basket to the other. The end person on the Pillow Case team carries it to the objects in the center. The player selects an item and holds it up for all to see. S/he then puts it in the case, saying the phrase rehearsed, such as *I place the flag in the pillow case.* With hand gestures of a choir director, the teacher directs the class response, *S/he placed the flag in the pillow case.* The player gives the pillow case to the next player and sits down.

A member of the opposing team then takes the basket to the center and chooses an item, saying, *I place the horse in the basket.* Everyone responds, *S/he placed the horse in the basket.* Students watch carefully, trying to remember which objects go in which container without making written notes. Students may not look in the basket or the case during the process. When all objects are in the containers, put the covered basket next to the closed case in the center.

On a blank sheet of paper, students write two column headings, ***In the Basket*** and ***In the Pillow Case.*** Under each, they list the items they remember. After students work individually for about ten minutes, have everyone consult a neighbor (on the left, right or wherever you stipulate) and compare lists as well as point out misspellings.

When the student pairs have finished making additions and changes (switching words between columns, for example), they count the total number of words and record it at the top of their papers. The pair doesn't have to agree.

The teacher then delivers handouts or students help themselves to the handouts listing the entire group of words in any order. You may add a few that were not in the game for extra challenge. Partners now correct spellings, make final changes and record the new count at the top of their papers.

When students have finished, the teacher reveals the contents of both the basket and the pillow case. Remove the items one at a time, alternating containers. Students check their lists as the items are revealed. Students subtract one point for each error from their total count.

If you wish to acknowledge the high scorers, say, *Raise your hand if you got more than ... (choose a medium number). Keep your hand in the air if you got more than ... (one number more).* Continue in increments of one until you get to the highest possible score. You might also note whether the Basket or the Pillow Case team had more high scorers, so that a winning team can be determined.

Variation One

To practice plural verb forms, *we* and *they,* students go in pairs to select an item. The partners place something in the container, saying, *we put...* The class responds, *they put...*

Variation Two

Younger students or those who do not yet know how to spell the words receive the handout as soon as items are in the containers. They refer to the handout when making their two columns, or more simply, direct them to circle the basket words and underline the pillow case words. This procedure is also appropriate for more advanced groups when speaking and reading comprehension are the goals. Less time is required for this version.

Guessing Games

Guessing games are excellent, low-anxiety ways to facilitate learning because the learners' knowledge of the language is not the focus. The answers are mainly determined by luck, logic and observation skills.

Who's in the House?

This versatile hiding game can be scaled down or up according to the level and ability of the group.

Purpose: Review of Nouns, Family, Phrases or Other Structures; Who or What Questions (Speaking, Reading)

Materials: Chalkboard; toy house, barn, boat or other container; objects small enough to fit inside container; blanket or towel large enough to cover container; paper bag or basket large enough to hold small objects

Procedure

Divide the class into pairs. Select a group of about 12 objects—miniature family figures and animals work well. The class tries to guess what the partners hide inside an interesting container, such as a toy house.

Two partners come forward and stand behind the toy house and basket of objects. The class names all of the objects as the pair takes turns holding them up. The teacher writes them on the board as they are named.

Cover the house with a blanket or large towel to facilitate the hiding process. The partners choose one of the items from the basket of objects and conceal it inside the house. The students remove the blanket from the house and place it over the basket. The teacher or one of the students asks, *Who's in the house?* If the object chosen is inanimate, the question is, of course, *What's in the house?* The hiders take turns calling on other students to guess, or guessing passes through the group in an established direction. During any silent time needed by the guessers, the teacher repeats the possible choices of the things listed on the board, *Is it the father, the mother, the sister, the uncle, the dog?* The guesser makes a choice, *It is (is it?) the ...* The hider responds, *Yes, It's the ...* or *No, it's not the ...* The teacher coaches throughout with possible questions and answers.

With each incorrect guess, one of the partners removes that object from the covered basket and holds it up to verify the meaning and show that it is not the one hidden in the house. The other partner is stationed at the board to check off the corresponding words as guessed. The person who guesses correctly and his/her partner earn the privilege of hiding the next object.

Variation One

To play the game competitively, divide the class into teams of four or five people each. A team is chosen to begin. Together they choose an item to hide and then select task assignments. One student removes objects from the basket to verify incorrect guesses. Another keeps score on the board, and a third crosses out the words as guessed. The fourth member asks the question, *(Name of team being addressed), who's (what's) in the house?* The fifth team member responds to the guess, *No, it's not... or Yes, it is...* The teacher coaches as needed on the correct lines.

Points are awarded to the hiding team according to how many guesses it takes the class to identify the object in the house. Each incorrect guess is one point for the hiding team. Guessing follows an established order, allowing one guess per team. The responsibility of guessing rotates within a team. Each team passes its mascot among members to keep track of whose turn it is to guess. When the object is guessed, the next team in line replaces the hiding team. Guessing begins with the team who is next in line to guess.

After all teams have had a chance to hide an object, a second round may be played, adding to the points accumulated by each team in the first round. The various tasks of the hiding team are rotated with each round. The team with the most points at the end of the completed rounds is the winner.

Variation Two

To increase the speaking skill level, assign more detailed descriptions to the objects. Expanded descriptions might include *the bald, 84-year-old grandfather, the cat who ate the mouse, the one-eyed pirate with a missing front tooth.* Take the time to dramatize a history for the props if the description is not observable as in *the cat who ate the mouse.* Board clues might still be simply the names of the objects, but guessers would be required to give the entire descriptive phrase.

Which One Will Be Last?

Students speculate on their classmates' moves in a game for beginning or advanced speakers.

Purpose: Review of Nouns, Adjectives, Adverbs, Verbs, Phrases or Other Structures (Speaking; Optional Reading, Writing)

Materials: 6 to 12 objects or pictures and a written description of each, container for collecting objects or pictures

Procedure

Display six to twelve objects or pictures in a line on the floor or chalkboard tray. Students' task is to remove the items one by one, but before the removal begins they predict which item will be removed **last** or remain in play the longest. The target vocabulary can require single word answers for objects, like *a dog,* or longer responses for descriptions of pictures, such as *a man running (runs) after a train,* or *the boy eating (eats) a sandwich*. Pictures can also depict adjectives, adverbs or verbs. Since drawings or pictures can be interpreted differently, make sure students understand your interpretation.

On a handout, the overhead or chalkboard, provide a written list of the choices. On a slip of paper, students write the description of the one they think will be removed last. If students do not read and write, or if you don't wish to emphasize writing, number or letter the items on the chalkboard tray or floor, instructing each student to record the number or letter of the item they select. After selections are made, students turn over their papers and put down pencils.

Two volunteers are each given a container, such as a basket or bucket. Students take turns naming items or describing pictures or objects for the collectors to put in the basket or the bucket. The teacher describes the remaining selection of pictures or objects repeatedly throughout the play. Those who correctly predicted the item which remains until last, yell, *I guessed it!,* or any other predesignated phrase.

Variation

To play competitively, divide the class into two or more teams. Students whose guess matches the last item earn one point each for their team. A graduated point system could be devised to include lesser points for predicting those which are among the last two or three removed.

If cheating by changing answers during the game arises, direct students to exchange papers with opposing team members. This information will provide some clues helpful in defeating the opponent. Do not allow them to discuss everyone's answers in an effort to play the best strategy, unless of course, it is done in the target language.

Teams alternate turns, asking the collectors (one from each team) to remove items from the chalkboard tray, one by one. Points are tabulated when all items have been collected. If time permits, play another round. Appoint a different student to the task of collector.

Mixed Category Concentration

New or review vocabulary pictures make an interesting team game involving both luck and skill.

Purpose: Introduction or Review of Nouns, Verbs, Adjectives, Adverbs, Phrases or Other Structures (Comprehension, Speaking)

Materials: 8 to 20 large picture flashcards in 2 or more categories (some duplication desirable)

Procedure

Students compete in teams to find and describe pictures which fit either subject categories (such as professions, sports and buildings) or grammatical categories (nouns, verbs, adjectives and adverbs). A group of 15 flashcard pictures should include no more than four categories. This game adapts easily to varying skill levels of different groups.

Any time new vocabulary is introduced, it is appropriate to spend time providing listening comprehension. In this first version, students need to be able to say the names of the categories, but not the items within them. See the variations for more advanced speaking.

The teacher introduces the flashcards by category, giving the description of each picture several times as the class examines it. More than one picture of the same item is desirable so that students have many opportunities to hear the new words. Shuffle the cards, then show and say them once again as you place them face down next to each other in any arrangement on the floor or on the chalkboard tray. If movement from students' seats to the pictures cannot be accomplished quickly, place pictures on the chalkboard tray and write a different number or letter above each card. Someone at the board turns over the cards according to the letters or numbers announced by seated students.

Write the categories, one each, on identical 3 x 5 cards. Divide the class into teams of four to six people. The first player chooses from the category cards which are offered face down. The player announces the category and turns over a picture or announces a letter or number for a student helper who turns it. The teacher describes the picture, holding and turning it so that all can see. If it is in the category announced, it is removed to begin the pile of points for that team.

If the flashcard is not in the named category, no point is scored and the card is removed to start a stack of incorrectly guessed pictures. These flashcards are returned to play when the original supply is exhausted. If you want play to pass more quickly, award incorrectly chosen cards to the opposing team. In the case of more than two teams, the card is awarded to the next team in line. Play continues through the teams as described. The team which accumulates the most flashcards is the winner.

Variation One

To review vocabulary, play a version requiring more speaking. Members of a team of three or four collaborate. Even though team members may help each other come up with the answers, one player (a different one each time) must take final responsibility for announcing the play and describing the picture. Two large teams are also possible. Assign partners or trios within each team for support.

A player names a category and the teacher gives descriptions of any two cards which are in that category. The student chooses one of the descriptions, announcing it before turning over the picture s/he thinks will match. If correct, the card is removed to begin the pile of points for that team.

If unsuccessful, the picture is offered to the next player on an opposing team. This time the teacher does not repeat the choice of descriptions, so an attentive team can gain the advantage. If a player declines the offer the teacher describes the card and turns it back over on the tray. That card remains out of play for at least one turn. The same player receives a choice of two more descriptions. Play continues in this manner.

Variation Two

In the most advanced speaking version, the game is played as described, except the teacher does not provide choices. Teams select pictures according to letters or numbers written above the card on the chalk tray. Collectively or with partners, they come up with descriptions in an effort to win the cards.

The teacher judges whether or not the team provides an acceptable description. If the team's description is inadequate, the teacher or other students help provide a better description and the card goes to the opposite or designated opposing team.

Telling Time

In the days of digital clocks, students may not understand analog (clock with hands) time-telling. Manipulating clocks helps them to understand the concepts as well as to maintain interest. Commercial clocks for teaching time are available from elementary curriculum catalogs or from learning stores. Homemade clocks are less durable but fun for students to make and use, and therefore often more effective.

Earlier or Later?

This activity is a non-threatening way to practice time since the competition is not to say the words correctly but to guess the leader's secret time.

Purpose: Telling Time, Adverbs of Time (Speaking)

Materials: Chalkboard, large clock

Procedure

Draw a twelve-hour time line on the board (see illustration). Label the left end 6 a.m. and the right end 6 p.m. Explain that 6 a.m. is the earliest possible time in this particular time frame and 6 p.m. is the latest.

The teacher sits facing the class, holding a clock so that others cannot see it. Position the hands on the clock at one of the times which the class has practiced, *2:15 p.m.*, for example. Ask a student to guess the time on your clock. Give less advanced groups some structure by announcing that the secret time is either 15 or 30 minutes past the hour. The student guesses, *(It is) 7:15 in the morning (a.m.)*. The teacher responds, *It is later than 7:15 in the morning.*

The next student now has a clue as to which direction to guess. S/he guesses a much later time *5 p.m. (in the evening)*, to which the teacher responds, *It is earlier than 5 o'clock in the evening*. The teacher continues, *What time is it?* responding, *Earlier* or *Later*, as the guesses are made. The guesses are verified by pointing them out on the board each time, but no marks are made.

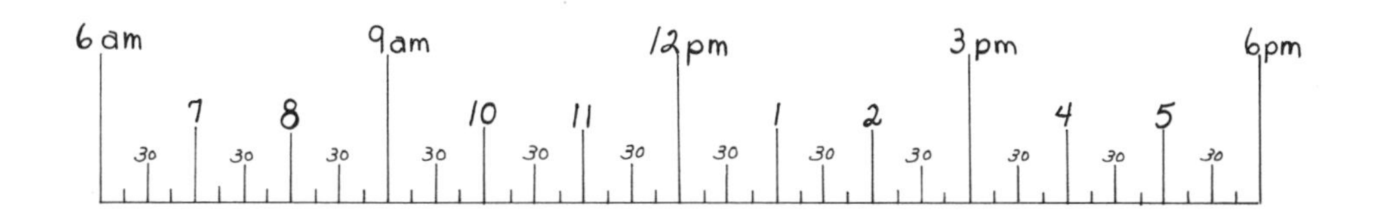

The student who arrives at the correct time of 2:15 in the afternoon takes the teacher's place and sets the clock on a different time. Guessing continues where it left off, and the student leader responds to each. At first, the student leader may be ready to answer only *Earlier* or *Later*, so that the teacher adds the more complete response, *It is earlier/later than...* *Before* and *after* could be substituted for *earlier* and *later*.

Variation One

For a team game, divide the class into three equal groups. One team sets the clock at an undisclosed time and the other two teams take turns guessing the time. Whoever is in charge of the clock holds it so only his/her team can see the time. After each guess, the responsibilities of responding *Earlier* or *Later*, as well as guessing the time, are rotated among team members. Passing a team mascot helps keep track of whose turn is next.

The first guess is worth six (or more) points, the second is five points, and so on until zero. If neither team guesses in the allowed number of turns, the clock-setting team receives the six points. The clock rotates to the next team and the other two teams take turns guessing.

Variation Two

Materials: paper plates, brads, felt markers

For pair or small group work, students make their own individual clocks from paper plates, using brads to attach the hands of construction paper or cardboard. Students compete within groups or in pairs in playing the preceding game.

Scream at Midnight or Laugh at 10:30

Overact when you model the actions to be performed at stipulated times. This encourages students to relax, enjoy and learn more easily.

Purpose: Telling Time; Commands; Present, Future and Past Tense (Listening Comprehension, Speaking)

Materials: Large clock, props that go with assigned actions

Procedure

Divide ten to twenty students into pairs and assign each pair an action and a time of day. One pair is to *cry at 2:30;* another is to *laugh at 9 o'clock.* Others sneeze, die, snore, hiccup, slam the door, honk the horn, pop the balloon or ring the bell, all at different times. Stipulate whether the time is a.m. or p.m. The complexity and number of different actions assigned will vary according to the skills of the learners. After parts are assigned, the actors come to the front of the room or stand so that everyone can see their actions.

Once on stage, the teacher double checks with the audience and actors to ensure that everyone clearly understands, *Who will snore? When? Who will kick the can? When?* This provides comprehension practice in the future tense and in speaking if students are required to give complete responses.

Set the hands of a large clock at one of the assigned times. Announce the time without showing the clock. The pair who were assigned 9 o'clock laughs loudly. If they do not respond, the teacher shows the time on the clock to prompt them. If able, students announce what they are doing as they perform the action. The teacher provides the descriptions in the comprehension stage.

To employ the past tense, ask questions about the actions that were performed. *When did (name of student and action)? Who snored? When? Who kicked the can? What happened at 6:30? What did (name of student) do and when did he do it?* It is better to wait a day or more after the performance to ask these questions. Then the focus can be on remembering who really did what, rather than questions asked just to drill the vocabulary.

Possessives

Since ownership is very important to most people, it is natural and interesting to teach possessive adjectives and pronouns with students' actual belongings or creations.

It's Mine (My)

Students have a good time and become better acquainted with their classmates as they try to match up people and belongings.

Purpose: First and Second Person Singular Possessive Adjectives or Pronouns; Nouns (Speaking)

Materials: Items which belong to students

Before the Game

All students are asked to bring to class a personal possession which does not reveal their identity. Written instructions are similar to this: *For Wednesday, bring to class a portable possession. Conceal it in an envelope, box or sack. We are going to play a game in which you try to match belongings with their owners.* You may want to restrict the assignment to clothing or other vocabulary upon which you are focusing. Encourage them to bring interesting objects. If some forget, have them use things from their purses, pockets and lockers, or perhaps provide an assortment of objects which they can temporarily own.

Procedure

The game is best played in a circle or two lines facing each other, but it is possible in rows. Divide the class into two equal teams, for example, the Chicks and the Ducklings. As a group, the Chicks take their items out of the room or out of view of the other team and remove any wrappers. The teacher also brings a possession and sends it out with one of the Chicks. The Chicks exchange items (all do not have to exchange, but most should). The Chicks return carrying each other's objects and place them in the middle of the circle on the floor or at the front of the room on a table.

The class watches and listens as the teacher inspects the collection. Pick up each item and comment on its beauty or utility, using the word several times with accompanying descriptive vocabulary. Students' opinions are welcomed to add humor and involvement. Chicks should be cautioned not to reveal ownership during the presentation of items.

At the end of the descriptions, each Chick takes turns claiming an item, either his/her own or someone else's. The Ducklings' task is to guess whether it really is the property of the Chick who claimed it. The teacher, who also has an item in the pile, models the procedure.

Picking up an item from the pile that **either does or does not** belong to him/her, the teacher says in a loud, dramatic voice, *This is*

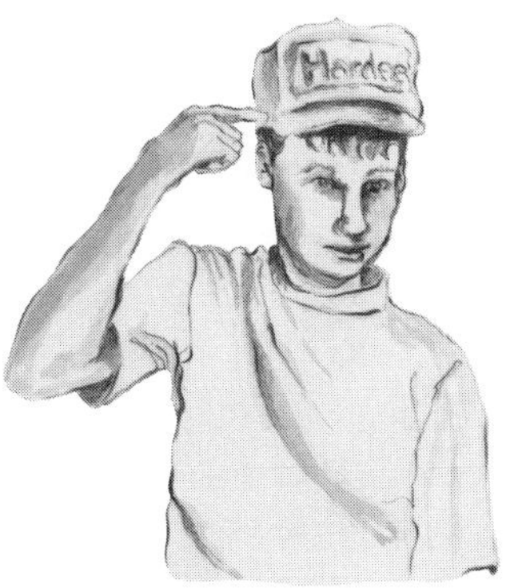

mine! or *This is my hat!* (Stipulate the use of either possessive adjectives or pronouns unless the group is ready for a review of both.) The first Duckling in line must decide whether or not the teacher is telling the truth and then either agree or disagree. Allow a simple *Yes* or *No* response or require that they give a more complete answer, such as, *Yes, it's your hat!*, or, *No, it's not your hat!* The teacher responds either, *You're right* or *You're wrong*. (Another *yes* or *no* response becomes confusing.) A correct guess earns a point for the Ducklings. If incorrect, the Chicks receive the point. (Do not count the teacher's turn unless the Chicks have one less player.) Points are recorded through marks on the board or beans in cups, etc.

The first Chick follows the teacher's model, holding up something from the pile and claiming to own it. Every time something does not belong to a Chick, it is returned to the pile for future selection. The Chicks take items with them when objects are identified correctly as belonging to them. After all Chicks have had a turn, the Chicks reveal who owns the remaining objects by claiming them truthfully, *This is my knife,* etc.

The Ducklings now take their belongings out of sight, exchange them, return, and place them in a pile. The teacher makes descriptive comments on the assortment. The Ducklings then take turns claiming the items. The team with the most points at the end of the two rounds is the victor.

It's Our(s)

The drawing takes extra time but stimulates student interest and creates reality.

Purpose: First Person Plural Possessive Adjectives or Pronouns; Nouns (Speaking)

Materials: Pens and paper for drawing

Procedure

This is similar to the preceding game, but students must create something in pairs or trios in order to create natural use of first person plural adjectives or pronouns.

Divide the students into two equal teams and assign pairs or trios within each. If possible, each team retreats to a corner of the room so the other team cannot easily observe them. If space does not allow separation of teams, students prop up books to shield their work from the other team. Provide colored pens and paper if possible. Each pair creates one drawing together. The subject of their drawing is any vocabulary which needs to be reviewed. Students could draw nouns, adjectives, adverbs, verbs, expressions of time, weather or a combination of these. The teacher may want to restrict students to one or two categories or sections of the text.

Avoid duplication of illustrations, yet allow students some choice in the words or phrases they illustrate. This can be accomplished by providing a numbered list with two or three choices per number. The teacher secretly (if both sides are given the same list) assigns every pair a different number and they may choose anything listed after their number. Team members may observe each other but not the opposing team. Students do not sign their names or use any distinguishing marks or styles that would give away the artists. Set a time limit if necessary.

Students place their finished drawings face down in a central pile for their team. The teacher selects the papers from one of the teams and displays and describes each masterpiece. The drawings are left spread out on the floor or table.

To begin the play, an artist pair comes forward and claims a drawing (their own or another). They present it to the first pair on the opposing team, saying together, for example, *This is our snowflake* or *This is ours.* The two opponents jointly decide if the artists are lying and answer, *Yes, it's your snowflake* or *No, it's not your snowflake.* The artists respond either, *You're right* or *You're wrong.* (Another *yes* or *no* response becomes confusing.) Pictures which are correctly identified as drawn by the claiming artists are removed. Others are returned to play. A correct guess earns a point for the artist team. If incorrect, the opponents receive the point.

When all artists have had a turn, the remaining drawings are claimed one by one, *This is our…*, etc. The teacher now describes the opposing team's creative works. They take turns claiming pictures and play continues as described. The team with the most points at the end of the guessing is the winner.

It's His/Her(s)

Students use their detective skills to figure out just what belongs to whom.

Purpose: Third Person Singular Possessive Adjectives or Pronouns, Nouns (Speaking, Reading, Writing)

Materials: Items which belong to students

Before the Game

Students each select an interesting possession to bring to class as described in the first paragraph of "It's Mine". Before the items are brought, each student writes a description of the item, five to ten sentences in length. Caution everyone not to reveal their items or descriptions to others. Check the written descriptions for mistakes and clarity.

Procedure

When descriptions are in good shape and the items are brought to school the game can begin. Divide students into groups of three to five people and choose team names. The groups should all be equal in number. Since there is a running competition among teams, interest is sustained even if the activity is spread out over several days. This allows rescheduling of teams with members who are absent or have forgotten to bring their possessions. Group members may show each other their items but do not reveal them to other groups.

Each group forms a huddle and chooses a team name. They secretly exchange objects and corresponding descriptions. Some team members may choose to keep their own. Each player rehearses the description which s/he will present. The group members help each other with unfamiliar words or pronunciations.

The first team to present are the Alligators. Each Alligator reads the description on the paper and shows the accompanying item. (It does not matter if the descriptions contain *my* or *I*.) The Alligators then sit down in the middle of the room with their possessions or stand facing the class behind a table where the items are displayed. The task of the remaining teams is to discern what belongs to whom.

Students direct their guesses to the teacher, not the presenting group. The teacher must know which item belongs to each Alligator. This can be accomplished either by preparing a list prior to play or by collecting the descriptions. The team first to guess is the Woodchucks. They each take one of the Alligators' five items and, in turn, place it in front of the person to whom they think it belongs. Each Woodchuck makes a statement as the item is placed with the person, for example, *It's her elephant. It's his glove. It's her pen. It's her picture.* For pronoun practice they would say, *This pen is hers. This glove is his, etc.* It is important that the guessers address the teacher, not the owners, in order to elicit the natural use of *his/her* (not *your*). The teacher notes how many are wrongly placed (not with the correct owner). If there are two incorrectly placed, the teacher says, *Two wrong,* and awards two points to the Alligators. No clues are given as to which three of the five items were placed with the real owners. The teacher or a student records the two points under the team name on the board.

The Foxes now come forward and collectively rearrange the items. Each Fox makes a statement about one of the items after the group arrives at a final decision. *(It's his glove,* etc.*)* The teacher again announces the number wrong, and the score (one point for the Alligators for every wrong guess) is added to the previous two points.

The Alligators' turn ends when the five items are finally in their proper places or when each team has had two attempts at rearranging the possessions, whichever comes first. The Foxes now come forward with their objects and descriptions. If the game is continued on another day, the teacher makes written note of the total score for each group, so that a winner may be declared after all teams have presented.

It's Their(s)

This game starts out with an activity for the right brain, an often neglected half of our thinking organ.

Purpose: Third Person Possessive Adjectives or Pronouns; Nouns (Speaking)
Materials: Art or craft supplies

Procedure

Elements of the two previous games, "It's His/Her(s)" and "It's Our(s)", combine to make a game using third person possessive adjectives and pronouns. Divide the class into teams of six and have them choose a name and a captain. Each person takes a partner within the team. (Uneven numbers can form trios.)

Students work in pairs to create something together. The product should be kept secret from the other teams, so separate the groups physically and visually as much as possible. The partners' collaborative creation can be any art or craft item which can be accomplished in a few minutes. They might draw a picture, fold and decorate a paper airplane, make a figure out of play dough or design faces on paper plates. Illustrations of vocabulary words, as described in "It's Our(s)", are also appropriate.

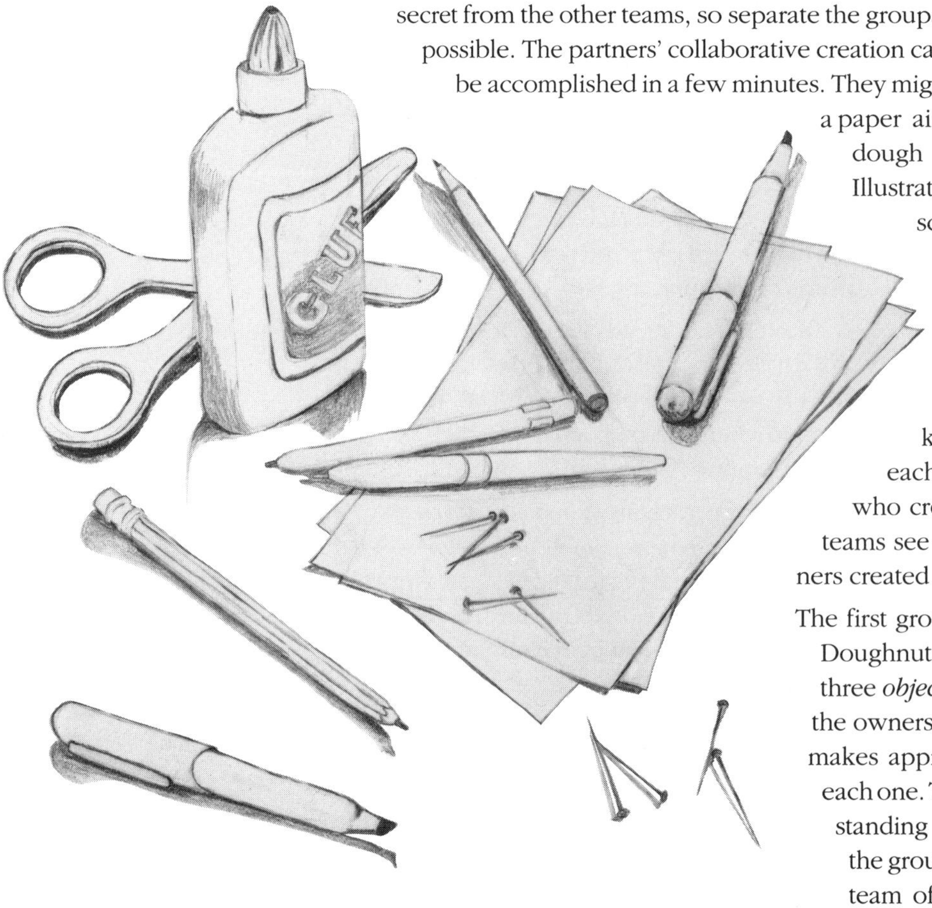

As soon as they finish, the students give the objects to their captains. The objects are not signed, so the captain makes a key for the teacher with the name of each object, followed by the partners who created it. It does not matter if other teams see the objects, as long as which partners created which items remains secret.

The first group to present their creations is the Doughnuts. The captain brings forth the team's three *objects d'art* (one by each pair) and gives the ownership key to the teacher. The teacher makes appropriate descriptive remarks about each one. The six team members face the class, standing or sitting with their partners behind the group of objects. Three people (half of a team of six) from an opposing team, the Muffins, arrange the items by giving them to or placing them directly in front of the creators. The three Muffins take turns announcing their guesses. *It's their rainbow. It's their dog. It's their paper hat.* To utilize pronouns, the guesses are phrased differently. *The rainbow is theirs. The dog is theirs. The paper hat is theirs.*

After the guesses are stated, the teacher announces the number of incorrect placements, and the Doughnuts receive two points for each wrong guess. The play passes to the Jelly Rolls and three of them come forward to rearrange the items. The Doughnuts' turn ends when the correct ownership is discovered or each team has had two turns, whichever comes first. If the Muffins or Jelly Rolls get a second turn, the three players who did not previously play do the arranging.

Play continues until all teams have been in the front of the class. The winner is the team which received the most points.

Games for the More Advanced

part 5

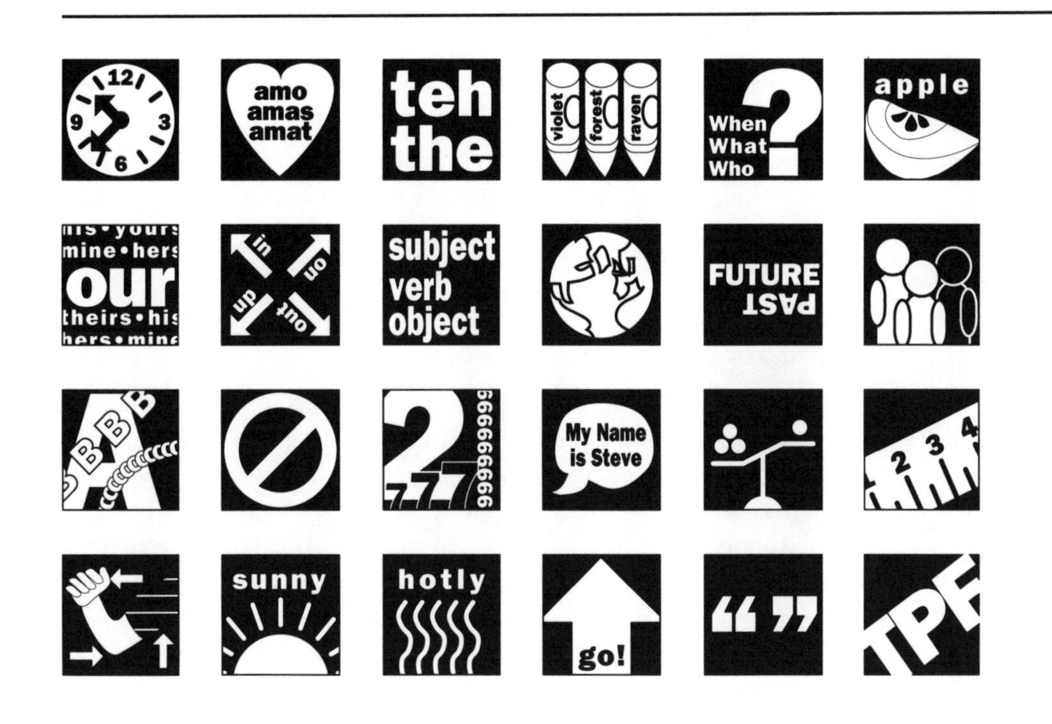

part 5 Games for the More Advanced

Adventures with Sentences

Students need activities with repetitive sentences as well as ones which allow creativity in producing their own messages. The following games provide both.

Spoken Gossip

Turn students' predisposition for whispering messages into a learning opportunity.

Purpose: Sentences, Phrases or Other Structures (Speaking)

Materials: An assortment of pictures or objects; 2 to 5 tape recorders (optional with small groups)

Procedure

Players whisper phrases or sentences to their teammates in chain fashion. The object is to pass the original sentences as accurately as possible.

Divide the class into groups of four to eight people seated in lines. The last person in each line should be someone who knows how to operate a tape recorder and who is a strong speaker. The tape recorder adds interest and serves the practical function of allowing the last person to immediately say and record what s/he heard rather than having to retain it until other groups have finished their turn. The tape recorder is not necessary if you have only one group.

Show the class one or more fairly detailed pictures in which various actions are taking place. Make several comments which describe the picture, for example, *The sun is shining; the dog is licking the cat; the boy is getting sleepy; the spider is chasing the fly.* The length and complexity of the description depends on the level of the learners. If you are targeting prepositions, you could make an arrangement of items on the floor or a table. Your comments match the arrangement, *The cat is in the hat, the tie is on the shirt, the flower is between the tree and the bird,* etc.

The teacher whispers a statement about the picture or objects to the first person in each group. Each student is to pass the statement on as soon as it is received, trying to reproduce, as accurately as possible, what was whispered.

Different statements of approximately the same length should be used for each group. If there are several groups, the teacher may need to write down, or have previously prepared the various statements given. Allow students to whisper the sentence two or three times if the receivers do not hear it well. No one may say the sentence to someone who is not immediately next in line. Upon arrival at the last person, the message is repeated aloud into the tape recorder.

After all have finished, the groups reveal in turn what the first person heard (teacher helps if it differs from what teacher whispered); then the last person plays the recording. If the command is not recorded, reverse the procedure: the last person says what was heard, then the first student (or teacher) relates the original. The entire class listens to the recordings and makes comparisons between beginning and ending statements for each group. The two can be written on the board for detailed examination. The goal is to transmit the statements without change, but the adulterated final versions can be very amusing as well as provide extended learning opportunities. If the activity is repeated, the students rotate positions within the group.

Variation

For a change of pace, students create commands to whisper through a chain of people. You may stipulate that they use a certain number of verbs or specific structures. In each group, the first person to have a command in mind sits in the starting chair. The command is passed and continues through the chain to the end person as before. Allow them to repeat the command whispered at least once.

The group is successful if the last person is able to carry out the command, such as, *Put on the flowered hat and sunglasses and kneel in front of the teacher.* Being the last in line is a good position for learners who can understand but are not yet ready to speak. If there are many groups, have the last person record or write down the command and wait until all groups have finished passing. The class watches as a command is carried out, then the other teams formulate what the command might be according to the student's actions. Lastly, the composer reveals what was initially said.

Reading and Writing Gossip

“ ” subject verb object

More sophisticated skills are required for this whisper caper.

Purpose: Sentences, Phrases or Other Structures (Speaking, Writing)

Materials: Paper and pencils

Procedure

Student groups collaborate to write sentences which they exchange and whisper though a chain of students. The challenge is to pass the sentences accurately from beginning to end.

Divide the class into groups of five to eight people each. Each group collectively composes a statement of seven to twelve words, depending on the ability of the group. You may require that they use certain vocabulary or structures or give them free rein. This activity could follow a discussion on a topic of interest. Their sentences would relate to the topic discussed.

One person in each group acts as secretary and writes the sentence on paper. When all have finished, the groups line up separately. The action can be observed best if the groups can face each other in a circle, square or rectangular arrangement. Leave a few feet of distance between groups if possible. The secretary stands at one end of the line with the sentence; the person at the other end needs a writing surface, a blank paper and a pencil. The secretaries exchange sentences so that each secretary has a sentence created by another group. No other player may read the exchanged sentences.

The secretaries are given one or two minutes to memorize the sentences. On a signal from the teacher, the secretaries turn over their papers and pass the messages on in whispers to the second people in line. Successive students continue the messages, whispering them to the people next in line. The students in last position write down what was heard. After all groups have finished, each group shares with the entire class the final product, then the original statement. As the two sentences are announced, the teacher or student can write them on the overhead or board to help make the comparison.

“ ”

subject
verb
object

Silly Sentences

This sentence-building activity calls for repetition and creativity, an effective, whole-brain combination.

Purpose: Sentences, Phrases or Other Structures (Reading, Writing)

Materials: Chalkboard

Procedure

Creativity needs some inspiration, so show the students a picture which has several interesting actions taking place. Ask students to describe the picture, allowing contributions of one or two words which the group builds into longer descriptions with the help of the teacher. Write some of the key words on the board.

The group is now to invent one long collective sentence. They may use any of the vocabulary discussed or may add words of their own. The sentence does not have to agree with the events in the picture. Everyone contributes a different part in the sentence composition.

For example, the teacher or a student provides a word or phrase to begin, such as, *The giant bubble, The wicked witch,* or *Suddenly.* Whatever is suggested is repeated orally by the class, then written individually on paper. The teacher or a student volunteer also writes the phrase on the board **after** students have attempted it on paper. Successive students add to the sentence with single words or phrases. With each addition, the group repeats the entire sentence in unison, ending with the latest component. The teacher directs the choral repetition with hand gestures.

When a contributor can think of nothing to add, the teacher asks for suggestions. When students make mistakes, the teacher simply changes it to correct form without directly pointing out the error. Encourage humorous combinations. The evolution of a sentence could look like this:

Cautiously,

Cautiously, the black

Cautiously, the black ghost

Cautiously, the black ghost sat

Cautiously, the black ghost sat on

Cautiously, the black ghost sat on a dead

Cautiously, the black ghost sat on a dead fish

Cautiously, the black ghost sat on a dead fish with

Cautiously, the black ghost sat on a dead fish with a worm

Cautiously, the black ghost sat on a dead fish with a worm in

Cautiously, the black ghost sat on a dead fish with a worm in its

Cautiously, the black ghost sat on a dead fish with a worm in its eye.

Variation

The students' collective creations provide interesting material for assigned dictation.

Secret Silly Sentences

A fun-filled adventure in collective writing of secret sentences focuses on both form and meaning.

Purpose: Sentences, Phrases or Other Structures (Reading, Writing)

Materials: Sentence strip or sheet of 8 1/2 x 11 paper per student

The group collectively composes sentences as in the previous activity. This time, however, everyone contributes every time and no one reads or knows the contents of the sentences until the end.

Before the Game

Before the game begins, the teacher gives several examples of sentences which follow a pattern such as this one in six parts: 1. Noun subject (who?) 2. Adverb (how?) 3. Transitive verb (action) 4. Object (what?) 5. Phrase of place (where?) 6. Phrase of time (when?). Examples include: *The President* *hungrily* *ate* *the pie* *in the kitchen* *after midnight* or *The frog* *swiftly* *catches* *flies* *in the air* *on a sunny day*. Other patterns can be substituted. The pattern must represent, of course, the normal word order of the target language. Have students brainstorm other sentences which follow the model you have chosen. Less advanced students will need to build a list of words and phrases in each division so that they may refer to them during the sentence writing in the game.

To prepare their papers, each student turns a sheet of notebook paper sideways so that lines go up and down. In the middle, they draw a single line across from side to side. This is the line on which students will write. Instruct the students to fold the paper in half (left to right) and then in thirds to make six equal parts (or the number of divisions in your sentence pattern). Number each space from one to six. This allots the appropriate space for writing each portion of the sentence. An option to notebook paper is sentence strips, long narrow lengths of paper available from supply catalogs for elementary schools.

Procedure

Establish a process for passing papers. A circular seating arrangement is best. If your class is arranged in rows, teach the group to pass from row to row in an S pattern. The first row passes back and the person on the end passes to the next row. The second row passes forward and the first person passes to the third row who passes back, etc.

Students begin their sentences by writing a subject noun at far left of the paper on the line or on the fold. The sentences are composed in secret so after each student writes the subject noun, s/he folds the number one portion over itself to prevent the next writer from seeing what was previously written. Everyone folds the paper over just enough so that what has just been written cannot be seen. Fold to the second column, not over it. Demonstrate where to write and how to fold.

The teacher writes on the board or privately gives any words which students need to see spelled. Less advanced students consult their prepared lists. Encourage use of adjectives to modify the subjects, such as, *The sleepy President* and *The green frog.*

When all have written subjects, everyone passes to the left, right, forward, or behind, as previously instructed. Each receiver holds the fold shut, and without looking at what has been written, writes an adverb on the line in the second column. Again, the teacher gives examples and spells any words students need. Students make another fold to conceal the adverb and pass again. Continue in this manner for the remaining columns, instructing students to write a verb which takes an object, a noun object (what), a place (where), and finally a time (when). Everyone passes after every addition. Prepositions are included whenever students think it is necessary.

After the time (when) is written, the sentence is complete and students pass one final time. Each unfolds his/her paper and reads the sentences silently for understanding. They now act as editors, making grammatical and spelling corrections or adding words if needed for syntax. Caution the editors not to change the meaning.

Students then share aloud the often hilarious results with the group. To extend learning and allow full enjoyment, the teacher repeats each sentence once with the help of the reader and again with the help of the entire class. Any other necessary grammatical changes are made by the teacher or suggested by the class. Examples which have been produced are as follows: *The mold hit the elephant happily in the closet last Wednesday. The pregnant mother eats roller skates noisily under the sink in summer.*

Variation One

Less advanced students may benefit by first playing this more structured version. Everyone composes one or more sentences on paper following the established pattern and using vocabulary the teacher stipulates. Students make vertical slashes between the various parts of the completed sentences and numbers them to make certain they have included the correct number of parts in the right order. Encourage students to help each other in the writing process, creating a more productive, collaborative effort. Collect the sentences for final correction.

For the game, return the papers, but not to the owners. The recipients read the sentences and consult the writers to be sure they understand the meaning of the sentences. On separate paper turned so the lines are up and down, each student draws a line across the middle and folds the paper in sections corresponding to the number of parts in the sentence. (See detailed description in the first version.) The noun subject from the sentence each received is copied on the line at the far left. The students fold the paper over, just enough to conceal what they wrote. They pass the folded paper to their neighbors (see passing discussion in the first version) but retain the papers with the full sentence. Students continue to copy from their papers, fold, and pass in unison. Each time, the teacher gives instructions as to what part of the sentence to copy. At the end, the editors make corrections and necessary additions. In turn, all share the results; they can be as hilarious as in the less controlled version.

Variation Two

When students understand the process, two or three sentences can be written, one under the other, on the same paper. (Students draw two or three lines on their papers.) Writers use different vocabulary in each sentence but follow the grammatical divisions of the pattern indicated by the teacher.

Conditional Capers

Students' perfectly sane sentences can become ridiculously funny with a little mixing of clauses.

Purpose: Compound Sentences with Dependent and Independent Clauses (Writing, Reading)

Materials: 2 colors of 3 x 5 file cards, 2 containers to hold cards, scissors

Procedure

This activity can be used to practice many compound sentence structures. The teacher provides a format within which students write responses. The first version is for *if* clauses. See Variation One for other possibilities.

Provide several examples of sentences that begin with an *if* clause such as, *If I had a million dollars, I would travel around the world; If I lost weight, my clothes would fit better; If I broke my arm, I wouldn't have to write my term paper.* A review of the tenses involved and dependent and independent clauses is appropriate. Students each write ten sentences using the structure described and hand in for correction.

Return corrected papers to the owners. Give each student two 3 x 5 file cards, each one a different color, for example, one blue and one white. Pass out scissors and have them cut each card into five equal strips, the long way. Students choose the five sentences they like best and write the first parts (the *if* clauses) on blue strips and the second clauses (conditional) on the white strips. The strips are collected and placed written sides down into separate baskets of blue ones and white ones.

Divide the class into two equal groups and provide each with one of the baskets. The student with the blue basket draws a blue strip and reads it aloud to the group. A student from another side chooses from the basket of white cards to complete the sentence. In large groups, start the baskets at points which will allow movement of the baskets to maintain the maximum distance apart. (If students are close in proximity, there is no need to speak loudly. See page 23, *Whose Turn Is It?*) The teacher and class repeat the combined parts of the sentence and ponder the meaning. The results range from logical to ridiculous and outrageous combinations. Students continue to draw and read the sentences until everyone has had a turn or time runs out. There will be too many to read on one day. Save the remaining strips and repeat the activity another time.

Variation One

Other possible clause combinations include *When I see* (student fills in description of an object or event), *it makes me feel* (student fills in feeling corresponding to first clause), such as:

When I see people exercising, it makes me feel tired.

After I..., I always... (After I do my homework, I always feel relieved.)

Since I..., I haven't been able to... (Since I got my driver's license, I haven't been able to afford any gas.)

I usually... because... (I usually don't watch television because there are few interesting programs.)

I never... when I... (I never ask for anchovies when I order pizza.)

I want to..., but... (I want to finish this book, but I keep rewriting it.)

Variation Two

To extend learning, use an overhead to write the sentences as they are announced. Use the more interesting combinations in a future test, or in a reading or dictation assignment.

Seeking Information

Too often students are given opportunities to answer questions and little opportunity to ask them. Learners can inquire about cultural, personal and general information in a variety of interesting ways.

Capture the Monarch

Taking prisoners makes this one popular. Interest is easily sustained for an entire class period.

Purpose: Forming Questions, Review of Cultural Information (Writing, Reading)

Materials: Multiple small objects for scorekeeping, paper crowns optional

Procedure

This activity is excellent for reviewing any information which the class has studied. Students' egos are less threatened, however, if the facts involved are personal or information not generally known.

Divide the class in two groups of monarchs—Kings and Queens. A boy/girl competition is effective and harmless if used infrequently. Don't worry if you have more girls than boys or vice versa; the groups do not have to be equal in size. If you choose genderless team names, divide the groups equally. The teacher assigns a category for the questions, such as personal information. On paper, all students write three to five questions about themselves, the answers to which only they or their team know. You may wish to stipulate that they begin with different question words, such as, *who, what, where, why, when, which, how,* etc. For each question, students make up two false but plausible answers and also include the real one. For example, *What is the natural color of my mother's hair? Red, Brown or Blond.* The writers underline or circle the real answer. Do not number or letter the answers, because students tend to respond with the letters or number rather than stating the complete answer.

Another category might be factual information which the class has studied together: *What is the capital of Spain?, Madrid, Barcelona or Grenada.* Team members should be encouraged to help each other write the questions, but warned not to discuss them with the opposing team. The teacher circulates, checking for mistakes and giving help. The teacher may wish to collect the questions, check for errors and return the papers for play the following day.

With questions in hand, Kings and Queens sit or line up opposite each other. Offer each group a paper crown if available. The crown rotates through the group and is worn by the players who are asking and answering the question. Since play moves from one side to the other, the crown helps the teacher and students keep track of the action. It is always the turn of the players with the crowns. (If you use team names other than Kings and Queens, have them pass a mascot.) You could also provide scepters (rulers) to pass. Start the two crowns at points which will keep movement of the crowns at the maximum distance apart. Talking to someone in close proximity invites speaking softly, preventing others from hearing. (See page 23, *Whose Turn Is It?*) Provide each team with a container and 10-15 fake or foreign coins (or any other small item you have in quantity) for scorekeeping.

A Queen begins by loudly reading her first question to the King. The teacher repeats the question during the silent time needed for the King to make a choice. If there should be an error in the question, restate it without focusing on the error. If the King answers the question correctly, the player records the point by putting a coin in the Kings' container. If the question is answered incorrectly, the King is taken *prisoner* by the Queens. He must go sit or stand in the Queens' territory. (Queens do not receive coins for the Kings' incorrect guesses.)

Crowns are passed and the next Queen asks her question to the next King. A correct answer always liberates a prisoner from the camp of the opponent. If there is more than one prisoner, the one who has been in captivity longest is always the one released first. Only when a winning team has no captives in the opposing team's camp are they eligible to win a coin.

If the King team is smaller than the Queens, some Kings will answer more than once, since each Queen must ask one question. When the Queens have finished questioning, any prisoners not liberated may return to the Kings' camp. Then the Queens must answer the Kings' questions and win points or lose members as described. Each Queen receives a question, so some Kings may have to ask more than once. At the end, any Queens in captivity are released and play may end or return to the Kings for another round. The winning team is the one which earned the most coins or if no one was awarded coins, the victor is the team which collected the most prisoners at the end of the round. Students mark the questions used and any unasked questions are collected for later use.

Variation

To focus on reading, members on the same team exchange papers and read each other's questions to the opposing team. Another exchange is made for the second round, after all players have read one question. Caution students against using *I, my* and *our,* since they are not the authors of the questions they read.

World Records

This triple-objective activity provides review of cultural information as well as practice in superlatives or comparatives, and question formation.

Purpose: Forming Questions, Review of Cultural Information, Comparatives, Superlatives (Writing, Reading)

Materials: Source books for information

Procedure

Students prepare five to ten questions about geography or any general cultural information which the class has studied. Give students a format for the question, according to whether you want them to practice comparatives or superlatives.

For superlatives, students write the question, then provide three answers. They might ask for the highest mountain, longest river, deepest body of water, age of the oldest living person, etc. For example, *What is the deepest underwater point on earth? Mariana Trench, Puerto Rico Trench* or *Death Valley*. One is the correct answer, and the other two are incorrect but plausible. Students circle or underline the correct answer on their papers. You may wish to stipulate that they begin with different question words, such as, *who, what, where, why, when, which, how,* etc. **For use of the comparative,** students ask a question containing a choice of two answers, such as *Which continent has more people, Europe or Africa?*

Students consult notes, texts or other sources to ensure they have valid information. If general or little-known facts are the assigned topic, *Comparisons* by the Diagram Group, *The Guiness Book of Records,* and *The World Almanac* are helpful and readily available at most libraries.

Use the questions (after correction) in a team game such as chalkboard baseball or football. Playing fields with bases or yard markers and goal lines are drawn on the board. A correct answer entitles the team to advance down the field or around the bases to score points. You may wish to expand the rules to include penalties or moves backward. Invite the students to help you formulate the rules.

In small groups, students can play commercial board games involving questions. For a special project, students create their own board games on paper. The teacher reproduces them for play in pairs or small groups. These questions could also be used to play "Capture the Monarch" or "Luck of the Roll".

Variation

An alternative to book information is to write personal questions (using the comparative or superlative form) on the characteristics of the class. Students seek information about other class members concerning height, weight, size of hands or feet, number of teeth, siblings, etc. of class members.

For superlatives, point out that questions do not all have to begin with who; there are other possibilities. *Who is the oldest? How much does the heaviest student weigh? When is the tallest person's birthday? In which town has John lived the longest? Why does Sally have the world's largest book bag? Where does the person with the biggest feet sit? What is the age of the youngest sibling in the class?* Be sensitive to students' egos. A question about weight, for example, is appropriate only for a class with no students who consider themselves overweight. Students write one correct and two incorrect but plausible answers for each question.

Comparative questions will be mostly *who* and *which* questions. *Who is taller, Martina or Pablo? In which class did Enrico get the best grade, geometry or tap dancing? Who can hold their breath longer, Gustave or Christian? Which makes Antonio more envious, a friend in a Corvette or a friend with a good-looking date?* Conducting investigations to find out the correct answers is part of the fun and learning.

Luck of the Roll

Luck and skill make a winning combination in this review activity.

Purpose: Forming Questions, Review of Cultural or Grammatical Information, Comparative, Superlative (Writing, Reading)

Materials: 3 x 5 cards, dice

When
What
Who

Procedure

Students prepare comparative and superlative questions as described in "World Records" or use any other question format and category for review. After students have written and corrected five or more questions and answers, they copy them individually on strips of sturdy paper or 3 x 5 cards cut in half the long way. The cards are mixed together and placed face down in a central deck, or the strips are put in a container.

Divide the class equally into two or more teams, the Bugles and the Trombones, for example. Each Trombone thinks of a number between 1 and 6 and writes it secretly on a piece of paper, then puts down his/her pencil. The teacher provides each team with a die. If a team is larger than ten members, they use two dice and choose numbers between 2 and 12.

The first Trombone rolls a 3 on the die. The Trombones then show their prerecorded numbers, and all those with a 3 must attempt a question. The Bugles take turns drawing and asking questions of the Trombones who wrote 3. If four people wrote 3, all receive a different question, one at a time. Any team member who had a 3 (but no one else) may help or give advice to any other 3. It is the luck of the roll if one of the 3's wrote the question drawn. Incorrectly answered questions are returned to the deck or container of questions; correctly answered questions are removed.

If no one has chosen the number rolled on the die, the same Trombone rolls again. Each correct answer earns advancement around the chalkboard or feltboard baseball bases or up a ladder, or any other goal. Creative point-scoring adds interest and extends learning. An example is to have teams compete to capture cities on a map of a country. When a team captures a city (gets five questions correct), they put their mark on the map at the site of the city.

After every Trombone with a 3 has attempted a question, play passes to the Bugles. The Bugles record numbers and roll the die. The Trombones take turns drawing and asking questions of all those matching the number rolled on the die. Players may not collaborate in choosing numbers. (This helps prevent the students from working out a system to skew the odds.)

Variation

The student objective and task of practicing question formation can be eliminated. The class can play "Luck of the Roll" strictly as review of information before a test, for example. The teacher creates and asks the questions.

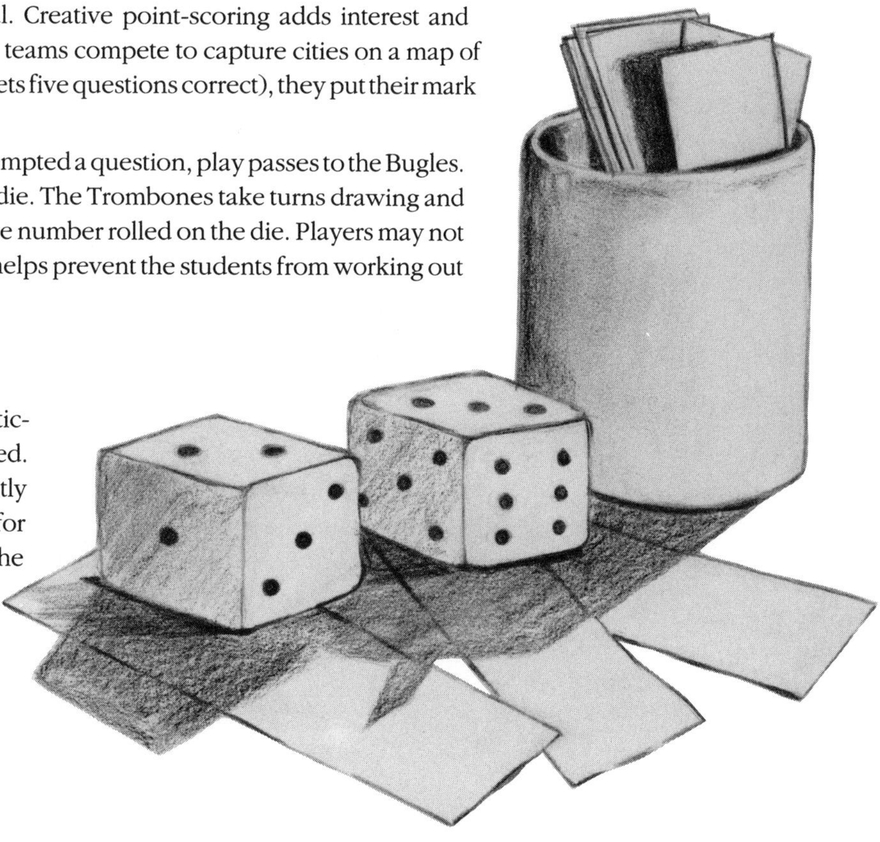

To Tell the Truth

Students question their classmates to detect who among them is lying.

Purpose: Questions and Answers, Negative Verb Formation, Phrases or Other Structures (Speaking)

Materials: 5 or more large picture flashcards, chalkboard

Procedure

This guessing game can be structured simply or made more advanced, according to the descriptions and flashcards chosen by the teacher. Divide the class into teams of five or six people. Show and describe five or six interesting pictures (the same number as there are members of a team) depicting objects, actions or situations, for example, *a rabbit jumping out of a hat, a dog running after a boy, a girl repairing her car, a monster with three heads* and *a boy making a cake.* (Make more detailed descriptions to increase the skill required, such as, *A boy making a frightful mess creating a three-layered chocolate birthday cake.* One team comes forward and stands in a line with their backs to the board, facing the class. The teacher assigns each one a number which they write above their heads on the board behind them. Each player receives one of the picture cards. Team members turn their backs to the class, form a huddle and exchange pictures. Taking care not to reveal the pictures, the five return to their places under the chalkboard numbers. If the pictures can be distinguished from each other by their different sizes or shapes, give each player a folder or envelope in which to conceal the picture.

The teacher selects any one picture for the class to find, for example, the boy making the cake. *Who is making a cake?* (or in more advanced vocabulary, *Who is making a frightful mess creating a three-layered chocolate birthday cake?)* A student begins the guessing, asking the first picture holder, *Number 60, are you making a cake?* Number 60 replies, *No, I'm not making a cake,* even if s/he does have that picture. The next guesser asks the second person, *Number 70, are you making a cake?* Number 70 answers, *No, I'm not making a cake.* All picture holders deny that they are making a cake as individually asked by different students. Students in the audience choose which number they wish to ask, but do not ask anyone who already answered. After a while, groups will naturally begin to experiment with different strategies in manner and tone in an effort to fool the class.

When all five have denied making the cake, the audience votes (according to the numbers assigned the players) by a show of hands for the one most likely to be telling the truth. Each member of the audience votes only once. The teacher asks, *How many think number 60 is (the one) really making a cake? How many think number 70 is really making a cake?,* recording on the board the number of votes which each team member receives. Then the players reveal their pictures one at a time, in random order (the real cake-maker goes last), showing and describing the picture they hold. The total number of incorrect votes is tabulated to determine the team's score. This number is posted under the team's name and previous scoring marks are erased. The next round requires a new group of liars and truth-tellers. Use the same pictures, minus the cake-maker, or a new set of pictures.

The team with the highest score wins.

Advanced To Tell the Truth

Students become better acquainted with their classmates in a playful competition to fool each other.

Purpose: Questions and Answers, Phrases or Other Structures (Speaking)

Materials: None

Procedure

This version of the preceding game is an excellent icebreaker and merits taking the time to do, even though it can take the better part of an hour, depending upon the size of the group.

Divide the class into teams of five to seven people. Have them choose team names. In a group meeting (out of hearing range of other groups) have all group members take several minutes to share an interesting or memorable event or other factual information about themselves. For example, Jim relates being the proud new owner of a long-awaited motorcycle; Diane tells what it was like to be a mother to a monkey, and Roberta relates being arrested for participating in a demonstration. Encourage them to give complete details and ask each other any questions they wish. The group then decides whose story could possibly be said about any of them and still be credible. They then decide how they will state it in one or two sentences. The statements do not have to be identical, just similar. Foreign language teachers have the option of accommodating less fluent groups by allowing students to have the discussion in English, then formulate the statements in the target language.

With statement in mind, the beginning group faces the class in a line-up. The teacher assigns ascending numbers for each position in line. Number 100 says, very convincingly, *I have a new motorcycle* (or whatever statement the group chose). Number 200 says, *I have a new red and black motorcycle.* One by one, the remaining group members make the same claim, varying their intonation and emphasizing different words for fun. In order to help pin down the truth-teller, the class members may take turns asking questions. For example, someone might ask, *Number 200, What brand is your motorcycle?*, or *How fast will it go?*

Set a limit on the number of questions according to how much time you have. After the questioning, the audience votes by a show of hands, and the number of votes for each person is recorded on the board. The teacher summarizes what the votes reveal, pointing out who the class believes is most and least likely to be telling the truth. Then the teacher says, *Will the person who really has a new motorcycle please step forward,* and Jim steps forward. The group may want to comment or ask more questions at this point. Incorrect votes are totaled to determine the team score. Another group lines up to tell their story. The winning group is the one with the most incorrect votes after all groups have presented their stories.

Biographical Fun

When students feel worthwhile, learning accelerates. This activity spotlights who they are and boosts self-esteem.

Purpose: Questions and Answers, Sentences (Listening Comprehension, Writing, Optional Spelling)

Materials: Biographical questionnaires

Procedure

This is a good activity to help the teacher get to know the students and for them to relate better to each other. Foreign language teachers have the option of doing this partially in the first language to accommodate less advanced students.

As homework, ask students to answer questions about themselves which you have prepared. Direct them not to work together or share their answers with anyone because you will use the answers in a guessing game about class members. Ask students to answer truthfully and leave blank any questions they feel uncomfortable with, rather than make up answers. Formulate the questions with the levels, backgrounds and interests of your students in mind. A sample questionnaire follows:

1. *What is your name?*
2. *Where were you born?*
3. *Where do you live?*
4. *Have you lived in another town, state or country? Where?*
5. *How many houses have you lived in?*
6. *How old are you?*
7. *What age would you like to be?*
8. *How many brothers and sisters do you have? Are they older or younger than you?*
9. *How long have you lived in your present house?*
10. *What is your favorite subject in school?*
11. *Do you like sports? If so, what is your favorite sport?*
12. *What is your favorite color?*
13. *Do you have any pets? What are they?*
14. *Do you have a special hobby or interest? What is it?*
15. *What do you want to do after you finish school?*
16. *Do you like school?*
17. *What season or month do you like best?*
18. *When is your birthday?*
19. *What is your favorite food?*
20. *If you were to take a trip to ..., would you go by train, plane, car, bus, boat or motorcycle?*
21. *Do you like to sleep?*
22. *How many hours a day do you sleep?*

23. *Do you like vegetables? Raw or cooked?*
24. *What is your favorite kind of ice cream? Cake? Pie? Candy? Fruit?*
25. *Do you watch television often? What is your favorite program?*
26. *Do you go to the movies often? Who is your favorite actor?*
27. *Do you like to read? What was the last book you read?*
28. *Where would you like to travel on a trip (anywhere in the world)?*
29. *If you had $1,000 to spend, what would you buy first?*
30. *Would you like to be the President of the United States?*
31. *Name a famous person, living or dead, whom you admire.*
32. *If you had to choose between being rich or happy, which would you choose?*
33. *Do you eat breakfast? What is your favorite breakfast food?*
34. *In which room of the house do you spend the most time?*
35. *Tell me something about yourself that you are willing to share and that hardly anyone else knows.*

Collect the results and keep them on file. Select one or two papers per class period, and read several questions and answers to the class in the target language (even if they have written them in English or their first language). Use actions and props to help clarify the meaning. After each person's description, ask students to write down on paper the name of the person they think you are describing. The person who is the subject must pretend s/he doesn't know. Guesses are announced at the end, before the true identity is revealed.

In order to build interest, start with descriptive information that will not be obvious. The students will not listen as intently if they know immediately who is being described. Don't try to include all the information on a person at one time. Mark those you use and save the others for another day.

Sources

part
6

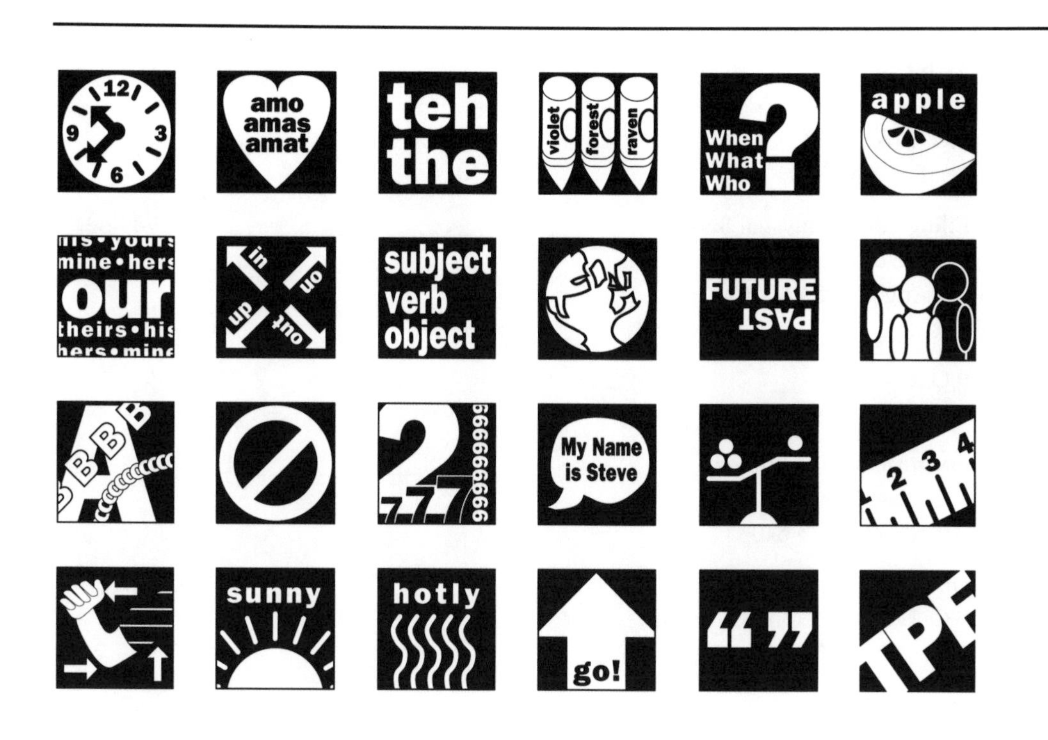
amo
amas
amat
teh
the
violet
forest
raven
When
What
Who
apple
our
subject
verb
object
FUTURE
PAST
My Name
is Steve
sunny
hotly
go!
TPF

part 6 Sources

Please note that addresses and telephone numbers are included for the convenience of the reader. These are current at time of publishing. Changes are beyond the control of the author.

Objects and Props

From Your Environment

Many common objects can be found in your own home or at thrift stores, garage sales, or through donations from students, parents, friends and relatives. Magnets, erasers and Christmas tree ornaments provide miniatures of many common objects.

From Mail-Order Catalogs

Catalogs offer a variety of materials including games, flashcards, realia, manipulatives, records, posters, cassettes and films. Each company specializes in different items. Catalogs are usually free on request.

Archie McPhee & Company ________ (206) 547-2467
3510 Stone Way North
P.O. Box 30852
Seattle, WA 98103

Bilingual Educational Services ________ (213) 749-6213
2514 South Grand Ave.
Los Angeles, CA 90007

Claudia's Caravan ________ (415)-521-7871
P.O. Box 1582
Alameda, CA 94501

Constructive Playthings ________ 1-800-255-6124
1227 East 119th St.
Grandview, MO 64030

DLM Teaching Resources ________ 1-800-527-4747
P.O. Box 4000, One DLM Park
Allen, TX 75002

Dormac, Inc. ________ 1-800-547-8032
P.O. Box 270459
San Diego, CA 92128-0983

Gessler Publishing Co. ________ (212) 627-0099
55 West 13th St.
New York, NY 10011

Ideal School Supply Company ________ 1-800-323-5131
11000 S. Lavergne Ave.
Oak Lawn, IL 60453

The Kiosk ____________ (408) 996-0667
19223 De Havilland Drive
Saratoga, CA 95070

Lakeshore Curriculum Materials Co. ____________ 1-800-421-5354
2695 E. Dominguez St.
P.O. Box 6261
Carson, CA 90749

Morrison School Supplies ____________ (415) 592-3000
304 Industrial Way
San Carlos, CA 94070

SUMO Publisher ____________ (608) 274-4880
1005 Debra Lane
Madison, WI 53704

Paper Props, Flashcards

Flashcards You Make

Collect old magazines and clip the advertisements that show something you wish to teach. The images are more interesting, colorful, current, and much less expensive than commercially produced flashcards. Christmas cards and calendars also depict a variety of objects and situations in eye-catching layouts. Glue the pictures on tag board to facilitate handling. (Colored construction paper is less durable and fades quickly.)

Flashcards You Buy

(See Also Mail-Order Catalogs)

Food Models

Life-size, color, photographic reproductions of common foods are available from your state Dairy Council. Visit or write your state Dairy Council or the National Dairy Council.
National Dairy Council ____________ (312) 696-1860, Ext. 220
6300 North River Road
Rosemont, IL 60018-1860

Drawings of Common Nouns, Verbs, Adjectives, etc.

Basic Vocabulary Builder and *Practical Vocabulary Builder* are blackline drawings for photocopying and provide innumerable uses.
National Textbook Company ____________ 1-800-323-4900
4255 West Touhy Avenue
Lincolnwood, IL 60646-1975

1000 Pictures for Teachers to Copy is another good source of line drawings. It also teaches you how to make your own.
Addison Wesley ____________ 1-800-447-2226
2715 Sand Hill Road
Menlo Park, CA 94025

Vocabulary and Grammar Manipulatives

These flashcards are written in symbolic fashion to capitalize on the power of the brain to remember through visual association. They are inexpensive because **you** color and laminate the designs.
The Color Connection
P.O. Box 13035
Arlington, TX 76013

TPR Student Kits

Peel-and-stick figures for students to manipulate at their seats are available from James Asher, the Father of TPR. Different settings are available, such as home, beach, farm, zoo, airport, grocery store and many more. Each includes ten lessons in English, Spanish or French. Obtain description of kits and other TPR materials from:
Sky Oaks Productions ________________ (408) 395-7600
P.O. Box 1102
Los Gatos, CA 95031

Posters *(See Also Mail-Order Catalogs)*

Authentic Advertisements

Old Poster Peddler
2820 Villageside Dr.
Santa Rosa, CA 95405

Promotion of Foreign Languages

Northeast Conference Posters
P.O. Box 623
Middlebury, VT 05753

Four-Color, Thematic

Subjects include sports, clothing, activities, transportation, animals, school and the kitchen, available in your choice of 15 languages. This company also carries holiday, poem and foreign language promotion posters as well as other materials.

éditions SOLEIL publishing inc. ________________ (416) 788-2674
P.O. Box 890
Lewiston, NY 14092-0890

In Canada:

éditions SOLEIL publishing inc.
P.O. Box 847
Wellend, Ontario L3B 5Y5
Canada

Miscellaneous

Game Pieces, Grammar Activities

Spinners and dice are useful for drill or games. Grammar activity kits include the subjunctive, past tense and reflexive verbs.

Toys and Tricks for Teachers ______________________________ (509) 747-6228
Margaret Herbert
S. 2930 Manito Blvd.
Spokane, WA 99203

Rubber Stamps

Written in French, Spanish, German, Japanese and Russian, these stamps can be used for decoration, paper-grading and recognition.

Sellos ______________________________ (503) 644-4902
4450 S.W. 107th
Beaverton, OR 97005

Bulletin Boards

Bulletin Boards with a French (or *Spanish) Accent* are books of ideas and visuals to create attractive and informative bulletin boards and include commentary on many topics. They also carry other decorative and motivational items.

Smile Press ______________________________ (608) 836-8048
P.O. Box 5451
Madison, WI 53705

Learning to Learn

They offer books, tapes and classroom units which include the latest research about human potential and learning for all ages. Whole-brain learning, critical and creative thinking skills, self-awareness, interdisciplinary curriculum, problem-solving.

Zephyr Press ______________________________ (602) 745-9199
P.O. Box 13448-A Dept. 40
Tucson, AZ 85732-3448

Audio-Cassette Magazines

Champs-Elysées, Schau ins Land, and *Puerta del Sol* are monthly magazines-on-cassette in French, German, Spanish and most recently, Italian. Each hour-long edition has news, features, popular music, interviews with celebrities and newsmakers, and tidbits of information about a variety of topics. A printed transcript of all spoken segments and song lyrics is included, complete with a glossary and cultural notes. All programs are recorded in Europe by professional broadcasters. Study supplements, priced separately, offer pre- and post-listening exercises based on selected program segments.

Audio-Magazines from Champs-Elyseés, Inc. ________________ 1-800-824-0829
P.O. Box 158067
Nashville, TN 37215-8067

Culture and Communication

Culturegram Series

Four-page briefings include information on topics such as social customs and courtesies, life-styles, geography, socio-economic statistics, history and government. The capsules cover 90 cultures. For sample Culturegram and complete catalog, send self-addressed, stamped envelope.

Brigham Young University Center for International Studies ______ (801) 378-6528
Publications
280 HRCB
Provo, UT 84602

Cultural News from Spain

Free monthly bulletins are available. Write for a subscription.

Revista "Información Cultural"
c/Torregalindo, 10-4a planta
28016 Madrid, Spain

Spanish-Language Magazine

A general interest, family oriented magazine designed for the Spanish-speaking community in the US. Published quarterly, an introductory two-year subscription is free.

Más ______ 1-800-955-3334
P.O. Box 025555
Miami, FL 33102-9825

French-Language Newspaper

This is an excellent general information source for teachers. Suitable for high school or adult classwork. Published bi-weekly. Write for a free sample.

Journal Français d'Amérique ______ 1-800-272-0620
P.O. Box 2516
Anaheim, CA 92825-5169

This Week in German

This newsletter is available at no cost.

German Information Center
410 Park Ave.
New York, NY 10022.

Annotated Bibliography

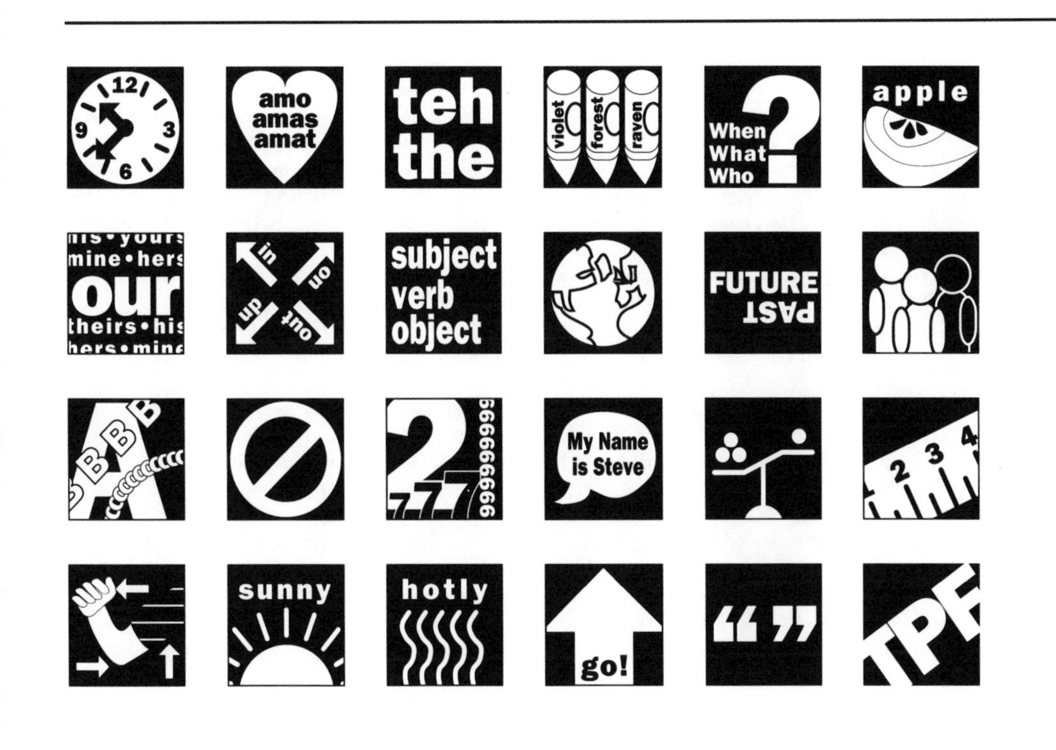

part 7

Annotated Bibliography

Please note that addresses and telephone numbers are included for the convenience of the reader. These are current at time of publishing. Changes are beyond the control of the author.

Books

1. Asher, James J. ***Learning Another Language Through Actions*** (expanded third edition), 1986, Sky Oaks Productions, P.O. Box 1102, Los Gatos, CA 95031. (408) 395-7600. Theory and practical application. The original Total Physical Response guide.
2. Blair, Robert W. ***Innovative Approaches to Language Teaching,*** 1982, Newbury House Publishers, A Division of Harper & Row, 10 East 53rd St., New York, NY 10022-5299. 1-800-242-7737. Anthology by authors in the forefront of innovative thinking about language teaching.
3. Burling, Robbins. ***Sounding Right,*** 1982, Newbury House Publishers (see #2 for address). An introduction to comprehension-based language instruction. Easy to read and convincing case in favor of the comprehension approach.
4. Canfield, Jack and Wells, Harold C. ***100 Ways to Enhance Self-Concept in the Classroom, A Handbook for Teachers and Parents,*** 1976, Prentice-Hall, Englewood Cliffs, NJ. Many of the activities are easily adaptable to language learning. High self-esteem is essential for successful language learners. For information about Canfield's seminars or ***Self-Esteem in the Classroom: A Curriculum Guide,*** write Self-Esteem Seminars, 17156 Palisades Circle, Pacific Palisades, CA 90272.
5. Curtain, Helena Anderson and Pesola, Carol Ann, ***Languages and Children – Making the Match,*** 1988, Wesley Publishing Co., World Language Division, Reading, MA 01867 (617) 944-3700. The definitive guide for establishing a FLES program. Research on curriculum, overview of key theory, objectives, rationale and practical activities.
6. Davalos, Diane. ***Activities to Expand Learning,*** 1984, Expanded Learning, 125 West Second Ave., Denver, CO 80223. A practical book of ideas for activities, games and skits.
7. Dhority, Lynn. ***Acquisition Through Creative Teaching,*** 1984, Center for Continuing Development, 64 Mountain St., Sharon, MA 02067. A beautiful blend of TPR, The Natural Approach and Suggestopedia.
8. Fluegelman, Andrew, Ed. ***The New Games Book,*** 1976 and ***More New Games,*** 1981, Doubleday and Co., Garden City, NY. Mostly games requiring a large space. Cooperative play for all ages.
9. Garcia, Ramiro. **Instructor's Notebook: How to Apply TPR For Best Results,** 1985, Sky Oaks Productions, Inc. (see #1 for address). Helps you become more accomplished with TPR.
10. Johnson, Roger and Johnson, David. ***Learning Together and Alone***, 1975, Prentice-Hall, Englewood Cliffs, NJ, and ***Circles of Learning,*** 1984, Association for Supervision and Curriculum Development, Alexandria, VA. Both are excellent guides for creating a cooperative environment. For a catalog of cooperative learning books, movies and videos, write Interaction Book Company, 162 Windsor Lane, New Brighton, MN 55112. (612) 631-1693. The Johnsons frequently present workshops. For further information write or call The Cooperative Learning Center, 202 Pattee Hall, University of Minnesota, Minneapolis, MN 55455. (612) 373-5829.
11. Krashen, Stephen D. and Terrell, Tracy D. ***The Natural Approach,*** available from Prentice Hall, 200 Old Tappan Rd., Old Tappan, NJ 07675. (201) 767-5937. 1-800-227-2375. Basic theory and practical application to get you thinking and doing.
12. Maley, Alan and Duff, Alan. ***Drama Techniques in Language Learning,*** 1982, Cambridge University Press, 32 East 57th St., New York, NY 10022. 1-800-872-7423. A resource book of communication activities for language teachers.
13. Moskowitz, Gertrude. ***Caring and Sharing in the Foreign Language Class,*** 1978, Newbury House Publishers (see #2 for address). A sourcebook on techniques to develop interpersonal communication once students have beginning conversation skills.
14. Seelye, Ned. **Teaching Culture,** 1984, National Textbook Company, 42555 West Touhy Ave., Lincolnwood, IL 60646-1975. Assists teacher and students in understanding culture and uncovering reasons why people behave as they do.
15. Van Oech, Roger. ***A Whack On The Side Of The Head,*** 1983, Warner Books, 666 Fifth Ave., New York NY 10103. Zeroes in on the mental locks that prevent you from being as innovative and creative as you can be. Shows you what you can do to open them.

16. Oller, John Jr., and Richard-Amato, Patricia A., Eds. ***Methods That Work,*** 1983, Newbury House Publishers, (see #2 for address). Description of a variety of communicative methods and ideas on how to implement them.
17. Orlick, Terry. ***The Cooperative Sports & Games Book,*** 1978 and ***The Second Cooperative Sports & Games Book,*** 1982, Pantheon Books. Good ideas for everybody-wins games. For some of the activities, you will need to add a language or speaking element.
18. Segal, Bertha. ***Teaching {English, French, Spanish, German} Through Action,*** Bertha Segal, 1749 Eucalyptus St., Brea, CA 92621. (714) 529-5359. Each text contains explanation of TPR and over 100 progressive lessons (ten units) in the target language for beginning level.
19. Smith, Frank. ***Essays Into Literacy,*** 1983, Heinemann Educational Books, 70 Court St., Portsmouth, NH 03801. Excellent insight into how people learn to read and write in the real world and how to recreate it in the classroom. Tapes containing his ideas are available from Abel Press, P.O. Box 6162, Station C; Victoria, BC, Canada V8P 5L5.
20. Weinstein, Matt and Goodman, Joel. ***Playfair,*** 1980, Impact Publishers, P.O. Box 1094, San Luis Obispo, CA 93406. Everybody's guide to noncompetitive play.
21. Winitz, Harris Ed., ***The Comprehension Approach to Foreign Language Instruction,*** 1981, Newbury House Publishers (see #2 for address). An anthology by major researchers who cover the theory and development of the comprehension approach .
22. Wright, Andrew; Betteridge, David and Buckby, Michael. ***Games for Language Learning,*** 1984 (new edition), Cambridge University Press (see #12 for address). Activities emphasizing communication and cooperation.

Journals, Newsletters and Professional Organizations

23. ***AATF National Bulletin,*** published four times a year by the American Association of Teachers of French. Contains information and ideas for teachers. AATF also publishes a journal (largely literary) six times a year. Both publications come with membership. Chapter treasurers can be found in the *French Review,* or send to AATF, 57 E. Armory Ave., Champaign, IL, 61820. (217) 333-2842.
24. ***AATG Newsletter,*** published five times yearly by the American Association of Teachers of German. A journal of pedagogy, *Die Unterrichtspraxis,* is published twice a year. The literary journal, *The German Quarterly,* appears four times a year. Membership includes the three publications. AATG, 523 Building, Suite 201, Rt. 38, Cherry Hill, NJ 08034. (609) 663-5264.
25. ***ADFL Bulletin,*** published three times yearly by the Association of Departments of Foreign Languages. Noted for surveys and coverage of professional and pedagogical issues. Regularly features essays on undergraduate and graduate curricula, creative approaches to teaching, technological developments in foreign language education, faculty development, international studies, and institutional and governmental policies concerning language study. ADFL Bulletin, Department A, 10 Astor Place, New York, NY 10003.
26. ***ALL Newsletter,*** published quarterly by the Advocates for Language Learning, an association of parents and educators working together to promote the study of second language and culture. ALL, P.O. Box 4964, Culver City, CA 90231. (213) 398-4103.
27. ***The Canadian Modern Language Review,*** published four times yearly (sometimes five). Partially written in French and includes articles and material of interest to teachers of all languages, at all levels of instruction. CMLR, 237 Hellems Ave, Welland, Ontario L3B 3B8 Canada.
28. ***DORS News and Notions,*** an inexpensive TPR and Delayed Oral Response Strategy newsletter containing ideas, activities, materials and conference information submitted by language teachers. DORS to Language, 44 Morningside Drive, Tiffin, OH 44883.
29. ***ERIC Clearinghouse on Languages and Linguistics News Bulletin,*** published twice yearly, sent **free** to subscribers of *TESOL Quarterly, Foreign Language Annals,* and the *Linguistic Reporter.* **Free** to others on request. Information on every aspect of language research and education and where to find it according to category. Send for free bulletin of available bibliographies, books, documents, computer searches and digests. Some are distributed for no charge. User services, ERIC Clearinghouse on Languages and Linguistics, 3520 Prospect St. N.W., Washington, DC 20007.
30. ***FLES NEWS,*** newsletter published by a National Network for Early Language Learning (NNELL). Facilitates communication among teachers of second languages to children, teacher trainers, parents, program administrators and policymakers. FLES NEWS, Gladys Lipton, NNELL, P.O. Box 4982, Silver Spring, MD 20914.

31. ***Foreign Language Annals,*** journal of the American Council on the Teaching of Foreign Languages (ACTFL), published six times annually, comes with membership in ACTFL. Articles on innovative and successful teaching methods, reports on educational research and experimentation, concerns of the profession. The ***ACTFL Newsletter*** is issued quarterly and contains news and notices about the organization as well as information about foreign language and international studies worldwide. ACTFL, 6 Executive Plaza, Yonkers, NY 10701. (914) 963-8830.
32. ***Hispania,*** journal of the American Association of Teachers of Spanish & Portuguese, four issues yearly, included with membership in AATSP. The journal is largely literary but AATSP publishes a newsletter, ***Enlace,*** which carries timely information of interest. Published three times a year. James Chatham, AATSP, Mississippi State University, Lee Hall 218, P.O. Box 6349, Mississippi State, MS 39762-6349. (601) 325-2041.
33. ***The Modern Language Journal,*** published four times yearly. Topics covered in MLJ include teaching strategies, bilingualism, applied linguistics, study abroad, innovative foreign language programs, developments in curriculum, teaching materials, testing and evaluation, and teaching of literature. Journal Division, University of Wisconsin Press, 114 North Murray St., Madison, WI 53715. (608) 262-4952.
34. ***NABE News, NABE Journal,*** published eight and three times a year, respectively. Included with membership in the National Association for Bilingual Education. Journal includes articles on instructional methods, techniques and research. Newsletter contains articles on bilingual education, updates on legislation and notices of conferences, jobs and publications in the field. NABE, Union Center Plaza, 810 First St. N.E., Third Floor, Washington DC 2002-4205. (202) 898-1829.
35. ***Northeast Conference Newsletter,*** published twice yearly. **Free.** Articles on successful teaching practices, teaching materials, news items pertaining to foreign language and international education. Northeast Conference on the Teaching of Foreign Languages, 200 Twin Oaks Terrace, Suite 16, South Burlington, VT 05403. (802) 863-9939.
36. ***On The Beam,*** newsletter published three times yearly by New Horizons for Learning, an international human resources network, comes with membership. Members receive discounts on NHFL-sponsored workshops, conferences. Excellent source for information relating to the human potential movement. NHFL, 4649 Sunnyside N., Seattle, WA 98103-6940. (206) 547-7936.
37. ***TESOL Quarterly and TESOL Newsletter,*** published by Teachers of English to Speakers of Other Languages, comes with membership in TESOL. Hands-on as well as theoretical information. TESOL, 1600 Cameron St., Suite 300, Alexandria, VA 22314. (703) 836-0774.

National/Regional Conferences

Many professional groups, as well as regional language associations, hold semiannual or annual conferences which focus on the effective learning of languages and encourage invaluable networking with colleagues. Programs and workshops include nationally known keynote speakers, presentations on successful teaching practices, culture, proficiency and evaluation. Vendors display the latest teaching materials and provide samples and ideas for implementation. Membership in the organization(s) entitles you to reduced conference fees. Many schools subsidize expenses to enable teachers to attend.

The American Council on the Teaching of Foreign Languages (ACTFL) can put you in contact with your state or regional language association (see ACTFL address listed below).

Regional associations include the Central States Conference on the Teaching of Foreign Languages, Middle States Association of Modern Language Teachers, Northeast Conference on the Teaching of Foreign Languages, Pacific Northwest Council on Foreign Languages, Southern Conference on Language Teaching, and Southwest Conference on Language Teaching.

American Council on the Teaching of Foreign Languages ________ (914) 963-8992
6 Executive Plaza, P.O. Box 1077, Yonkers, NY 10701-6801
(Publication–see #31 in Bibliography).

American Association of Teachers of French ________________ (217) 333-2842
57 E. Armory Avenue
Champaign, IL 61820
(Publication–see #23 in Bibliography)

American Association of Teachers of German ________________ (609) 663-5264
523 Building, Suite 201, Rt. 38
Cherry Hill, NJ 08034
(Publication–see #24 in Bibliography)

American Association of Teachers of Spanish ________________ (601) 325-2041
James R. Chatham, Executive Director
Mississippi State University
Lee Hall 218, P.O. Box 6349
Mississippi State, MS 39672-6349
(Publication–see #32 in Bibliography)

Advocates for Language Learning ________________________ (213) 398-4103
P.O. Box 4964
Culver City, CA.
(Publication–see #26 in Bibliography)

National Association for Bilingual Education ________________ (202) 822-7870
Union Center Plaza, 810 First St. N.E., Third Floor,
Washington DC 2002-4205. (202) 898-1829.
(Publication–see #34 in Bibliography)

New Horizons for Learning ____________________________ (206) 547-7936
4649 Sunnyside N.
Seattle, WA 98103-6940
(Publication–see #36 in Bibliography)

Teachers of English to Speakers of Other Languages __________ (703) 836-0774
1600 Cameron St., Suite 300
Alexandria, VA 22314
(Publication–see #37 in Bibliography)

Subject and
Grammar
Index
part
8

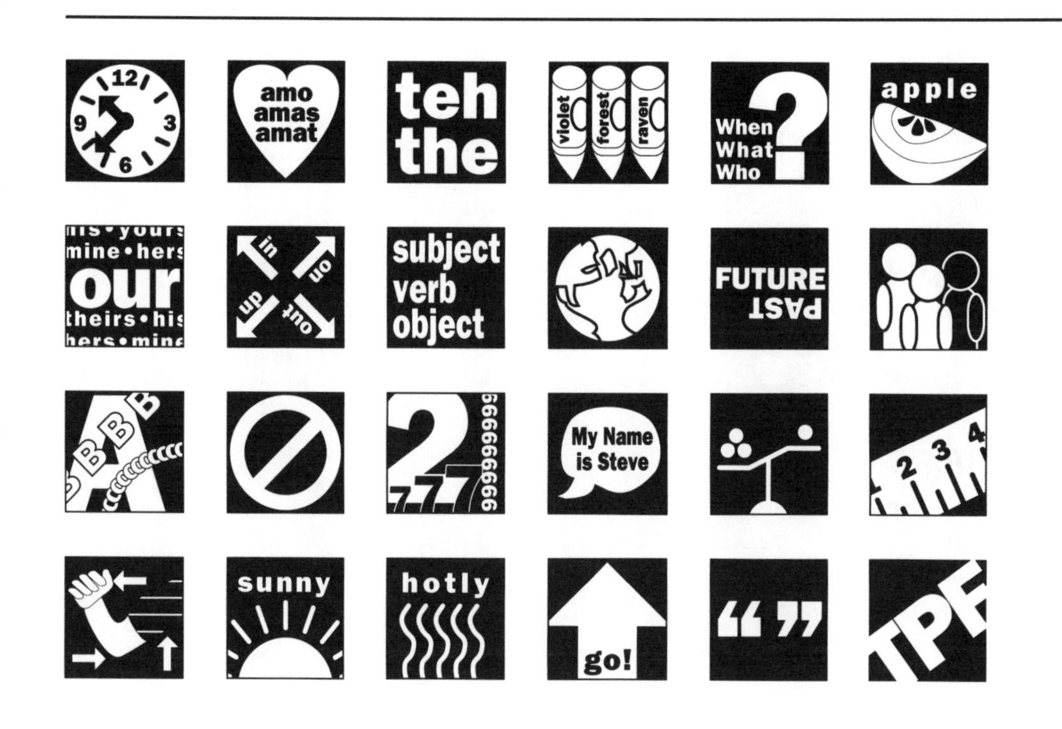
12
9
3
6
amo
amas
amat
teh
the
violet
forest
raven
When
What
Who
apple
his • yours
mine • hers
our
theirs • his
hers • mine
in
on
up
out
subject
verb
object
FUTURE
PAST
My Name
is Steve
2 3 4
sunny
hotly
go!
TPF

part 8 Subject and Grammar Index

Under each heading below, the games are listed in the order they appear in the book (from less to more advanced).

Adjectives

Adverbs

Alphabet

Body Parts (See Also *Nouns*)

Colors (See Also *Nouns*)

Commands

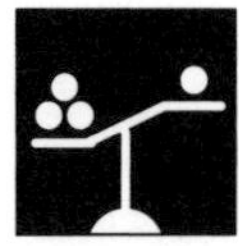

Comparatives and Superlatives

Cultural Information (Review of)

Family (See People)

Measurements and Adverbs of Distance

Names

Negative (See Also *Verbs*)

Nouns (See Also *Body Parts, Colors, Numbers, People*)

Nouns (continued)

Numbers **(See Also *Nouns*)**

People **(See Also *Nouns*)**

Phrases or Other Structures

Possessive Adjectives and Pronouns

Prepositions

Questions and Answers

Sentences

Spelling

Telling Time

Verbs

Conjugations or Infinitives

Tense

Alphabetic Listing of Games

part 9

Under each heading below, the games are listed in the order they appear in the book (from less to more advanced).

Alphabetic Listing of Games – continued

Improve Your Skills

For any of us who have spent years developing teaching behaviors that failed to produce proficient language users, it is not easy to take the difficult path of learning new or different ways. An effective prescription for growth is to figure out what you want to do by informing yourself; then seek out those who do well what you want to do and observe how they do it. Modeling of effective teaching can be found in colleagues' classrooms as well as in workshops and conferences.

Another element important to growth is the experience of different perspectives. In the case of teaching, it is necessary to know what it feels like to be a learner. A close examination of language teaching techniques includes an experience in learning language, focusing on what works for you and comparing it to what works for other learners in the class.

Finally, you must take the necessary risk and try out some of those techniques and procedures which attracted you. This is the most difficult step, and you must keep in mind that growth is not achieved through doing everything right. If you're not feeling uncomfortable and not making mistakes now and then, you're not growing. You know it's working when the act of doing sends you charging off in search of more information and more good modeling in order to do more testing and refining. Fortunately, it's a never-ending process which becomes increasingly more rewarding and less frustrating as you tap abilities you didn't know were within you.

Workshops Offered

In the series of workshops by Jo Ann Olliphant, *Methods That Work,* participants have the combined experiences of being language learners, observers of effective models, and teachers.

Teachers learn how to convert research into reality through demonstration and practical application of brain, learning and second-language research.

For more information on the *Methods That Work* series of workshops, write or call: Jo Ann Olliphant, 11004 111th St. S.W., Tacoma, WA 98498. Phone: (206) 584-7473.

ORDER
TPF

Ordering Information

Sahmarsh Publishing
11004 111th St. S.W.
Tacoma, WA 98498
Tel. (206) 584-7473

Please send me the book of strategies and activities for teaching and learning language through cooperative play, ***Total Physical Fun***.

Name ____ Phone ______________
Address ____
____ Zip___________

☐ Enclosed is a check or purchase order for **$24.95** plus **$2.50** shipping: Total **$27.45**.
Washington residents add **$1.95** sales tax: Total **$29.40**
For each additional book, add **$1.50** shipping.
Total number of books ordered________. Total payment enclosed________.
I understand that I may return the book for a refund within 30 days if not totally satisfied.

☐ Please send me information on workshops by Jo Ann Olliphant.

- -

Ordering Information

Sahmarsh Publishing
11004 111th St. S.W.
Tacoma, WA 98498
Tel. (206) 584-7473

Please send me the book of strategies and activities for teaching and learning language through cooperative play, ***Total Physical Fun***.

Name ____ Phone ______________
Address ____
____ Zip___________

☐ Enclosed is a check or purchase order for **$24.95** plus **$2.50** shipping: Total **$27.45**.
Washington residents add **$1.95** sales tax: Total **$29.40**
For each additional book, add **$1.50** shipping.
Total number of books ordered________. Total payment enclosed________.
I understand that I may return the book for a refund within 30 days if not totally satisfied.

☐ Please send me information on workshops by Jo Ann Olliphant.

Ordering Information

Sahmarsh Publishing
11004 111th St. S.W.
Tacoma, WA 98498
Tel. (206) 584-7473

Please send me the book of strategies and activities for teaching and learning language through cooperative play, ***Total Physical Fun***.

Name ______________________________________ Phone ______________
Address ____
____ Zip__________

☐ Enclosed is a check or purchase order for **$24.95** plus **$2.50** shipping: Total **$27.45**.
Washington residents add **$1.95** sales tax: Total **$29.40**
For each additional book, add **$1.50** shipping.
Total number of books ordered_______. Total payment enclosed_______.
I understand that I may return the book for a refund within 30 days if not totally satisfied.

☐ Please send me information on workshops by Jo Ann Olliphant.

- -

Ordering Information

Sahmarsh Publishing
11004 111th St. S.W.
Tacoma, WA 98498
Tel. (206) 584-7473

Please send me the book of strategies and activities for teaching and learning language through cooperative play, ***Total Physical Fun***.

Name ______________________________________ Phone ______________
Address ____
____ Zip__________

☐ Enclosed is a check or purchase order for **$24.95** plus **$2.50** shipping: Total **$27.45**.
Washington residents add **$1.95** sales tax: Total **$29.40**
For each additional book, add **$1.50** shipping.
Total number of books ordered_______. Total payment enclosed_______.
I understand that I may return the book for a refund within 30 days if not totally satisfied.

☐ Please send me information on workshops by Jo Ann Olliphant.